Ignatius
of Loyola

LEGEND AND REALITY

Ignatius
of Loyola

LEGEND AND REALITY

PIERRE EMONET, S.J.

TRANSLATED BY

Jerry Ryan

EDITED BY

Thomas M. McCoog, S.J.

SAINT JOSEPH'S UNIVERSITY PRESS

PHILADELPHIA

ISBN 978-0-91610-191-6
Library of Congress Cataloging-in-Publication Data
Names: Émonet:, Pierre, 1936– author. | McCoog, Thomas M., editor.
Title: Ignatius of Loyola : legend and reality / Pierre Emonet, S.J. ; translated by Jerry Ryan ; edited by Thomas M. McCoog, S.J.
Other titles: Ignace de Loyola. English
Description: Philadelphia, PA : Saint Joseph's University Press, 2016. | Includes index.
Identifiers: LCCN 2016036441 | ISBN 0916101916 (hardcover)
Subjects: LCSH: Ignatius, of Loyola, Saint, 1491–1556. | Jesuits—Spain—Biography. | Christian saints—Spain—Biography.
Classification: LCC BX4700.L7 E4613 2016 | DDC 271/.5302 [B]—dc23
LC record available at https://lccn.loc.gov/2016036441

Cover image: *The Consolation of St. Ignatius of Loyola* (detail). Oil on copper. Mexico, 18th century. Philadelphia, Saint Joseph's University Collection.

Cover design by Carol McLaughlin, Creative Services, Saint Joseph's University
Book design by Scribe Inc., Philadelphia

Published by
Saint Joseph's University Press
5600 City Avenue
Philadelphia, PA 19131
www.sjupress.com

Saint Joseph's University Press is a member of the Association of American University Presses and the Association of Jesuit University Presses

TABLE OF CONTENTS

Preface to the English Translation

Thirty years ago Philip Endean, S.J., adapted the question Jesus famously addressed to his disciples "Who do you say I am?" (Mk 8:29) to Ignatian studies: "Who do you say Ignatius is? Jesuit Fundamentalism and Beyond."[1] Pedro de Ribadeneira, S.J., author of the first biography of Ignatius: *Vita Ignatii Loiolae, Societatis Iesu Fundatoris* (Naples, 1572), provided younger Jesuits who had no personal knowledge of their founder, with a model to shape their formation, and presented this founder and his new religious order as valid and orthodox to quell lingering doubts about each. Numerous authors, Protestant, Catholic, agnostic, Jesuit and non-Jesuit have supplied multiple answers to Endean's question. In the twentieth century, at least one English biography of Ignatius appeared each decade. Over time, we have Ignatius the mystic, Ignatius the spiritual leader, Ignatius as Don Quixote. We encounter him as a heretic, as the founder of the Society of the Society. He is a doctrinaire papalist who wrote rules for thinking with the Church, and advocated blind obedience. He was called a disciple of the devil, a Machiavellian. He is a pilgrim in tears, eager literally to follow in the Lord's footsteps. The iconography is equally varied. Ignatius appears as an orthodox priest in a simple chasuble. He is seen in a simple black soutane holding a book, usually without a title or with only A.M.D.G. In the years preceding his canonization he was often shown as a miracle-worker. As the Society became a Counter-Reformation force, he smites heretics in Prague with his trident or presides over the destruction of their books in Rome. Today he is portrayed most frequently as a pilgrim, a person on a quest. But his years as a pilgrim were significantly fewer than those spent at his desk in Rome as an administrator, an armchair pilgrim delighting in the missionary journeys of his disciples.[2]

Ribadenira recognized that Ignatius can not be separated from the Society. No other miracles were required, according to Ribadeneira, because the very existence of the Society demonstrated his sanctity. "Si monumentum requiris, circumspice," the epitaph of Sir Christopher Wren proclaims triumphantly. Yes, look around. The Society of Jesus revealed Ignatius's greatness as St. Paul's, London, disclosed Wren's skill. Consequently biographies of Ignatius tend to be large, expansive, and inclusive. We learn much about his "life and times," the state of the Church, the Reformation, the missionary enterprise of the Society etc. Fascinating topics, often intriguing told, occasionally with pedantic detail. But the man gets lost.

The original French edition of Pierre Emonet's *Ignatius of Loyola: Legend and Reality* was published in 2013 by Éditions Lessius. It has since been translated into Spanish and German. Here we offer an English translation by Jerry Ryan, a freelance writer and translator of Antoine Arjakovsky, *The Way: Religious Thinkers of the Russian Emigration in Paris and Their Journal, 1925–1940* (Notre Dame: University of Notre Dame, 2013) and Hyacinthe Destivelle O.P., *The Moscow Council (1917–1918): The Creation of the Conciliar Institutions of the Russian Orthodox Church* (Notre Dame: University of Notre Dame, 2015). Why, given all the biographies, did the editorial committee decide to publish this one? Unlike many biographies, this is succinct without being superficial. Here one encounters Ignatius, the man and the legend, in almost Hemingwayesque simplicity. Here one sees the traits and characteristics that have attracted, annoyed, alarmed and amused generations. Perhaps we offer this as a prolegomenon, aperitif, to encourage further reading.

The editorial committee has adapted the text for an English-reading audience. As far as possible we have converted the references to more accessible texts, and have added a few passages of explanatory material. But the most obvious adaptation is the addition of a complementary "Life of Ignatius of Loyola in Images." This consists of fifteen images selected from among eighty-one copper engravings executed by Jean-Baptiste Barbé (1578–1649)—who enlisted the young Peter Paul Rubens (1577–1640) to contribute drawings for the project—for the 1609 illustrated biography of St. Ignatius of Loyola (*Vita beati patris Ignatii Loiolae*), published to celebrate his beatification that year by

Pope Paul V. The engravings reproduced here are from the copy of this work in the Jesuitica Collection at Saint Joseph's University, Philadelphia. Saint Joseph's University Press commissioned Ursula Hobson to hand-color these engravings to illustrate Father Emonet's biography. Each engraving is accompanied by an English translation, rendered by the late James P.M. Walsh, S.J., of the Latin caption explaining the episode from Ignatius's life that is illustrated. Father Walsh's translations were originally published in *Constructing a Saint Through Images: The 1609 Illustrated Biography of Ignatius of Loyola*, introductory essay by John W. O'Malley, S.J., Latin captions translated by James P.M. Walsh, S.J. (Philadelphia: Saint Joseph's University Press, 2008). In these engravings we see the metamorphosis of Ignatius from reality to legend as the Society advanced the cause of his canonization.

Thomas M. McCoog, S.J.

Notes

1. *Studies in the Spirituality of Jesuits*, 19/5 (1987).
2. See "My Own Personal Ignatius," posted on *Thinking Faith*, July 30, 2012 (http://www.thinkingfaith.org/articles/20120730_1.htm, accessed on August 12, 2016).

INTRODUCTION

In his *Life of Don Quixote,* Miguel de Unamuno, who was trying to reestablish the image of the wandering knight, wrote: "[I]t is in the light of death that one must look at life. . . . the ancient maxim which says 'As the life has been, so the death will be' . . . should be changed to read 'As the death is, so the life was.'"[1] If the philosopher is right, then it must be said that the life of Ignatius of Loyola was very ordinary indeed because his death was ordinary, as his secretary Juan de Polanco (1517–1576)[2] wrote in a letter to Pedro de Ribadeneira (1526–1611):[3] "He left this world the way we all do."[4] Ignatius died alone on July 31, 1556, without pathos, without convoking his companions to leave them a spiritual legacy, without the papal benediction he hoped to receive, without even finishing his life's work, *The Constitutions of the Society of Jesus*, entrusting the future to the Holy Spirit and to the practical wisdom of those who would succeed him

Did this ordinary death put a final seal on an ordinary life? In this case, absolutely not. The life of Ignatius was anything but ordinary. Few personalities have been as loved or hated as the founder of the Society of Jesus. For some, he was the genial organizer of a new form of religious life, an intrepid defender of the papacy, a charismatic practitioner of spiritual discernment, an apostle who took many initiatives even to the ends of the world such as it was known in those times, the precursor of a new style of evangelization which was open to modernity; but, for others, he was a calculator with a military mentality whose strength was a strict concept of discipline; he was a friend of the great and the powerful of this world, an ambitious man, thirsting after power and political influence, the organizer and leader of haughty and self-sufficient circles, the partisan of a voluntarist asceticism which constrains people and deprives them of poetry, a tyrant over submissive souls which are subjected to fastidious examinations of a narcissistic accountancy, a mystic who flirted with unaccountable inner illuminations, a rationalist who demystified the Christian mystery, an inquisitor financed by the Vatican and the chief of an army of mercenaries at the service of the pope, the originator of situation morality and casuistry, an amateur of double-talk . . . and God knows what else. So it is that, in the course of time, a twofold legend was woven around this man who had a very ordinary death but who was anything but an ordinary man. The Golden Legend and the Dark Legend dispute the true portrait of Ignatius of Loyola. Each can cite irreproachable saints, scholars, elites, ecclesiastical and secular, philosophers, intellectuals, and writers as witnesses. Each side numbered wise men, first class intellectuals, e.g., Pascal, Descartes, and Voltaire, politicians, gifted authors, statesmen, theologians, emperors, revolutionaries, and defenders of the status quo, popes, churchmen, believers and disbelievers. The praises which Ignatius aroused are only equaled by the criticisms of his detractors. The first celebrated his teachings; the other denounced them. Some esteemed him as a providential personality who opened Europe to modernity; others accused him of introducing the ferment of modern heresies into Europe. For some he was a Reformer; for others, a Counter-Reformer. He was a staunch defender of the faith for some; the gravedigger of Christianity for others.[5] Whether they were fascinated or indignant, enthusiastic or disappointed, his critics and admirers dispute his reputation and legacy. Most criticism comes from non-Jesuit observers who narrate raw facts without putting them in a context which would make it possible to discover their signification. They hardly bother to read his autobiography, spiritual journal, or any of his correspondence.[6] It is true that certain companions who had lived with him, specifically Simão Rodrigues (1510–1579) and Nicolás Bobadilla (1511–1590), had described him as authoritarian and accused him of favoritism and ambition. In their desire to propose an ideal image of the founder to counter that presented by his critics, Jesuit chroniclers and witnesses of his daily life at Rome (Luis Gonçalves da Câmara [1520–1575], Polanco, Ribadeneira) did not always avoid the snares of hagiography. Carried away by their affection and admiration for him and perhaps influenced by internal quarrels and ecclesiastical harassments, they painted a very edifying portrait.[7] There is also the fact that history has projected many of the posterior defects of the Society on to Ignatius; rather than passing judgment on him, it passed judgment on the Jesuits insofar as they strayed from the ideal presented by their founder.[8]

Where is the truth in all of this? How can the real Ignatius be rediscovered above and beyond the ambiguous personage which all too often haunts the popular imagination? An excursion through the sources in order to hear his own memories, to gather the testimonies of his closest companions, to listen to the confidences of his spiritual journal, and to scrutinize some of the innumerable pages he wrote, will enable us to advance a bit and approach the person behind the personage created by tenacious legends, both gilded and darkened. The autobiographical account which he dictated to his colleague Gonçalves da Câmara between 1553–1555 will serve as our main theme. Approaching the end of his life, Ignatius did not want to draft a simple collection of random memories. At the insistence of his companions, he reread his own story to find the ways the Lord had led him. By handing over his own itinerary, he left them a sort of foundational testament.

The diversity of opinions regarding Ignatius is explicable, in part, by the fact that a critical observer could recognize in him some traits which were not without a certain ambiguity: the constant tension between individual liberty and fidelity to the institution, between the particular and the universal, between the ideal and real. On the one hand, Ignatius respected the person as the place where the Spirit manifests itself, and he thus constantly defended the possibility of a person having an immediate experience of God, without any intermediary; on the other hand, he gave priority to the more universal good, and his respect for ecclesiastical and political institutions made him a firm supporter of the Sovereign Pontiff as a person whom princes and kings could take into their confidence. For Ignatius, contrary to the old adage, the letter—i.e., the institution—gave the spirit flesh and blood, inserted it into the world with the subsequent dangers and risks of compromise. His faith in the Incarnation obliged him to affirm the two extremes. Most miss this. By preferring the legends, they fail to account for the complexity and magnanimity of relations between God and humans.

Notes

1. *Our Lord Don Quixote. The Life of Don Quixote and Sancho with Related Essays*, trans. Anthony Kerrigan (Princeton: Princeton University Press, 1967), p. 306.

2. Juan de Polanco, a close collaborator and the right hand man of Ignatius, was an excellent organizer and administrator who became the secretary for the Society in 1547—a function he would continue to exercise under the next two superior generals.

3. Pedro de Ribadeneira wrote the first official biography of Loyola in 1572. A translation by Claude Pavur, S.J., was published recently: *The Life of Ignatius of Loyola* (St. Louis: The Institute of Jesuit Sources, 2014).

4. Polanco to Ribadeneira, Rome, August 6, 1556, *Fontes narrativi de S. Ignatio de Loyola et de Societatis Iesu initiis* (4 vols.; Rome: Institutum Historicum Societatis Iesu, 1943–1965), vol. 1, p. 768. In the original French edition, the author cites Ignatius of Loyola, *Écrits* (Paris: Desclée de Brouwer, 1991) throughout. We have converted the citations to accessible English editions,

or, in the case that an English translation does not exist, to the original documents in the *Monumenta*.

5. See John W. O'Malley, S.J., "Was Ignatius of Loyola a Church Reformer? How to Look at Early Modern Catholicism," and "The Many Lives of Ignatius Loyola: Future Saint," in *Saints or Devils Incarnate? Studies in Jesuit History* (Leiden: Brill, 2013), pp. 71–87, 257–97.

6. See Pierre-Antoine Fabre, "The Writings of Ignatius Loyola as Seminal Text," in *A Companion to Ignatius of Loyola*, ed. Robert Aleksander Maryks (Leiden/Boston: Brill, 2014), pp. 103–22.

7. See Philip Endean, S.J., "Who Do You Say Ignatius Is? Jesuit Fundamentalism and Beyond," *Studies in the Spirituality of Jesuits*, 19/5 (1987); Robert Aleksander Maryks, "The Quest for the Historical Ignatius," in Maryks, *Companion*. pp. 1–4.

8. On this see Rafael Olaechea, S.J., "Historiografia ignaciana del siglo XVIII," in *Ignacio de Loyola y su tiempo*, ed. Juan de Plazaola, S.J. (Bilbao: Mensajero, 1992), pp. 55–105.

I

A Basque Gentleman

The Family Soil

Íñigo López de Loyola[1] was born in 1491 into a world undergoing a profound transformation. The following year, Christopher Columbus would extend the frontiers of the known world, and provide Spain with an empire on which the sun never set. In Europe, the Middle Ages were ending to be replaced by the new paradigms of the Renaissance.

Íñigo was the youngest of 14 children; 8 boys and 5 girls had preceded him, two or three of which were illegitimate. Their father, Don Beltrán Yánez and his spouse, Doña Marina Sáenz of Licona, belonged to the *parientes mayores*, the provincial nobility, land owners of extensive domains, who lived from their lands and on their lands. Rich and often haughty, they constituted a privileged class in Guipúzcoa, one of three Basque provinces in Spain; powerful and respectable, they were capable of opposing the king. Two rival clans, the Oñaz and the Gamboa, disputed control of the region to the detriment of social and political life. The Loyolas were related to the Oñaz. To assure their power and fortune, these *parientes mayores* ruled arbitrarily, even resorting to sowing terror, ransacking villages, assassinating without scruples until the cities organized a resistance to them. King Henry IV of Castile, weary of these internal quarrels, had their fortified towers, symbols of their arrogance, razed, and exiled the ringleaders to Andalusia to fight against the Moors. The grandfather of Ignatius was among these.

Don Beltrán had served the kings of Castile who rewarded him well by granting him substantial annual rents from the foundries of Barrenola and

Aranaz as well as the right of patronage over the parish of Azpeitia whose taxes would now be paid to Beltrán. Doña Marina, exhausted by her numerous pregnancies, was unable to nourish her youngest son who was entrusted to a wet nurse in the house of María de Garín, the solid and pious spouse of the blacksmith Errazti who lived in the nearby village of Eguíbar. It was surely in the house of the blacksmith that Ignatius babbled his first words in Basque and was initiated into the popular usages and customs of his country. Until the end of his life, he would talk about how the chestnuts tasted, about regional dances and folk songs. But it was in the big family house that he received the rudiments of his formation under the tutelage of some beneficiary of Azpeitia. There he learned to read and write and was taught the rudiments of grammar and Latin. From this first formation, history has retained the excellent quality of his calligraphy.

His father and his elder brother Martín accompanied him as he progressed, but it was above all Martín's wife, Doña Magdalena de Araoz, who had the greatest influence on his initial education. Having lost his mother at a very early age, Ignatius always cherished Magdalena as his second mother.

From a religious point of view, Ignatius was an ordinary Christian, practicing regularly, professing the Catholic faith and obedient to the Church. While still a child he received the tonsure and, consequently, found himself integrated into the "clergy" of the diocese of Pamplona, a privilege he would later exploit to escape civil justice and to obtain authorization to travel in the Holy Land.

A Frivolous and Censured Youth

But, all the same, the ecclesiastical world offered less interesting perspectives than a career at the royal court where someone could gain the favor of the king and other elites, and achieve glory in battle. There was no lack of examples in his own family. Several of his brothers attained fame while in the king's service, or left Spain to seek glory in far-off military expeditions. Admission to court as a page constituted a more promising future than the study of Latin and grammar. But, nonetheless, it was still necessary to obtain a recommendation from some noble in good-standing at court. A distant relative, a friend of his father, Don Juan Velázquez de Cuéllar, *Contador maior* (chief treasurer) of the king, offered to accept Íñigo into his service as a page, promising him lodging, food, a family atmosphere, and the guarantee of an education harmonious with his rank and aspirations. Thus it was that in 1506, the young Íñigo, 15 years old, left his homeland for Arévalo, near Ávila in Castile. Juan Velázquez received him with a great deal of affection and treated him like one of his own sons.

Íñigo spent 11 years with Velázquez, practically all of his youth, a time when he finished his gentleman's education and learned the customs of the court. Although it was a sumptuous and luxurious life, the morality was, nonetheless, austere, according to the Castilian mentality, and the education he received was perhaps more serious than at the paternal mansion. Íñigo, who was an excellent dancer and an amateur musician, learned to play a stringed instrument, perhaps an early form of the violin; in the jousts and tournaments he proved to be courageous. Even though he was not a bookworm, he found writings in the palace library which nourished his ideals. One notable discovery was *Amadis of Gaul*, the late-medieval collection of tales of romance and chivalry, which fascinated him with its stories of the exploits of the chevaliers. These were years of trouble, however, marked by "the vanities of the world" and "offenses of the flesh."[2]

What was this "going astray, typical of young people"? Shady stories of women, quarrels decided at sword point, perhaps even an illegitimate child.[3] Again examples were not lacking in his own family. Don Beltrán, his father, his older brothers Martín and Pedro, the future parish priest of Azpeitia, had all fathered several illegitimate children. In a letter in which he evoked his memories of the founder, Diego Laínez (1512–1565),[4] a close companion and successor as general superior, wrote that Ignatius had been assaulted and vanquished by vices of the flesh until the moment he made a vow of chastity, Henceforth the Lord gave him the gift of chastity.[5] Polanco, who supplemented the memories of Laínez, recalled that before his conversion, Ignatius did not live according to the faith he professed, but was particularly addicted to games, to women, and to the use of weapons. In order to excuse him and preserve the reputation of the holy founder, the good secretary added that Íñigo did this "by force of habit."[6]

A lawsuit which took place in Azpeitia concerning events on the night of of Mardi Gras, 1515, bears witness to this troubled period. Íñigo and his brother Pedro were accused of several serious offenses whose nature was not specified. The sentence, however, alluded to very grave wrongdoing, committed after dark, intentionally, during an ambush.[7] Íñigo, who remembered he had previously been tonsured and fearful that his career might be compromised by this crime, fled to Pamplona, and placed himself under the protection of the bishop. The judge, Miguel Vernet, was not at all intimidated by ecclesiastical privileges and pointed out to Íñigo that his lifestyle was a thousand miles away from the clerical state and that his behavior was indeed scandalous. Moreover, instead of wearing the clerical habit and a decent tonsure, he walked around fully armed, his hair down to his shoulders and dressed in multi-colored vestments. Three years later, in 1518, Íñigo was again threatened by a certain Francisco de Oya who wanted him dead—to the point of bribing a woman Íñigo was seeing to murder him at his next visit. The reason? Doubtlessly another conflict among chasers of skirts.

The companions of Ignatius, who were more uncomfortable about his past than was Ignatius himself, tried to ignore it. The friendship and admiration they had for him led them to suggest that he skip over the more disedifying incidents of his youth. In order to preserve the ideal image of the founder, his first companions did not hesitate to censure the narrative gathered by Luis Gonçalves da Câmara from 1553 onwards where Ignatius related his whole life and the errors of his youth "clearly and distinctly with all the circumstances."[8] It is very improbable that Câmara himself censured what Ignatius told him. On the other hand, there are indications confirming that the manuscript had been mutilated. Ten years after the death of the founder, Ribadeneira explained to Jerónimo Nadal (1507–1580)[9] that Francisco de Borja (1510–1572),[10] the third Superior General of the Society, ordered that all copies of the autobiographical narrative then circulating within the Society be sent to Rome, and prohibited its reading by Jesuits and outsiders.[11] This was a veritable impoundment whose avowed purpose was to avoid any contradiction between the oral narrative of Ignatius and the new biography assigned to Ribadeneira, intended for the edification of Jesuits. For the spiritual sons of Ignatius, this was a prudential measure in view of the canonization of the Founder. It was better to forget the episodes which could be of interest to the Inquisition. Silence about this troubled past seemed all the more justified since, at that time, Father General Borja was regarded as suspect by the Inquisition. Pushing prudence to its extreme limit, Ribadeneira related Ignatius's youth in very vague and general terms, while omitting passages which could be understood as sympathetic to Erasmus or to the *alumbrados*.[12]

The manuscript of Luis Gonçalves da Câmara remained on shelves in Rome until it was discovered by the Bollandists[13] in 1731, with a part of the introduction and the chapter where Ignatius tells of the follies of his youth amputated. The first steps of a gilded legend!

THE AMBITION AND GALLANTRY OF A SOLDIER

The death of the king of Spain, Ferdinand the Catholic (1452–1516), on January 23, 1516, and the accession to the throne of the youthful Charles I (and later Holy Roman Emperor Charles V [1500–1558]), brought about the disgrace of Juan Velázquez. Soon after he lost his position and influence, the ex-chief treasurer died from chagrin and resentment. This came as a severe shock to Íñigo, a real tragedy. With his protector's fall from grace, the whole environment which was propping him up and was the source of his revenues came collapsing down, seriously compromising his career and his future projects. The generosity and the mediation of María de Velasco, widow of his protector, provided a solution to the situation. Armed with her recommendations and fortified with a generous viaticum of 500 écus and two horses, he offered his services to the viceroy of Navarre, Don Antonio Manrique de Lara, Duke of Nájera (d. 1535), a Spanish grandee. Since this brilliant Basque gentleman, allied with the Oñaz, might be able to gain the favor of the inhabitants of Guipúzcoa, the duke gave him a friendly reception.

Íñigo was 26 years old. His entry into the service of the viceroy in 1517, marked an evolution in his itinerary. Without referring to it as a first conversion, he began a more organized life. Up to that point Íñigo, "given over to the vanities of the world,"[14] had not done much of anything with his life. From now on, he would pursue the serious life of an ambitious, courageous, and righteous soldier, of a gentleman pursuing a career. As a member of the household of the duke, he accompanied his noble protector when he went to meet the young Charles I at Valladolid. It was doubtlessly on this occasion that he caught sight of the young sister of the king, the Princess Catalina, whose beauty and sweetness would haunt his most impossible dreams for a long time.

As Polanco has pointed out, Íñigo was skillful and prudent, capable of handling delicate and difficult situations. As a wise negotiator, with a gift for calming dissensions, he successfully conducted negotiations which led to the pacification of Guipúzcoa. For Polanco, these natural qualities prefigured the great things he would later accomplish for God, even if, at that time, he did not always put his natural talents and skills at the service of good causes.[15]

Everything changed dramatically on Pentecost Monday, May 20, 1521, during the siege of Pamplona, when a ball from a French cannon shattered the legs of Íñigo who was the mainstay of the defense of the fortress. He had arrived two days earlier with his brother Martín at the head of a Basque contingent. The young officer refused to turn back when the city, which was in the grip of an internal quarrel in which French partisans seemed to have the upper hand, told them that their services were not wanted. Martín, disgusted, left the city along with a good part of his troops. Íñigo, cut to the quick, "thought that it would be shameful to also withdraw like that and, motivated by his great courage and his ambition for glory, he left his brother planted there and, spurring on his horse, he went galloping back to the city with a small group of soldiers."[16] The viceroy had abandoned the city, leaving a lieutenant, Don Pedro de Beaumonte, in charge. Íñigo, holed up in the fortress, was determined to defend it even to death in spite of the lack of motivation on the part of the defenders who spoke only of surrendering. He refused any compromise. For him, things were clear: either vanquish or die for king, honor, and glory. With this determination, he obstructed the negotiations which the *alcalde* of the fortress, Miguel de Herrara, was conducting with the French in the hope of arriving at an honorable solution. His obstinacy and courage won out over the defeatism and political prudence of the lieutenant, but not over the fire power of the French artillery. A bombardment fractured his right leg and seriously damaged the other.

The fortress, the core of the defense on the ground, was taken. Along with the bitter taste of defeat, the proud gentleman, who excelled in the art of combat and gallant undertakings, was stricken in his physical integrity. A dream would fall apart for the hero and another adventure would begin. His first Jesuit companions always dated the true birth of their founder, Íñigo of Loyola, as May 20, 1521.

Notes

1. Íñigo (Ennecus in Latin) was the name given at baptism and the name he would use in Paris (cf. chap. IX).

2. *Saint Ignatius's Own Story*, trans. William J. Young, S.J. (Chicago: Loyola Press, 1956), pp. 3 num. I, 11 num. 10.

3. Even though they do not amount to absolute proof, historians have uncovered various indications that insinuate that Ignatius had fathered a child during his turbulent youth. See José Martínez de Toda, S.J., "María Villarreal de Loyola, ¿Presunta hija de Íñigo de Loyola? (Los Loyola de la Rioja del S. XVI)," *Archivum Historicum Societatis Iesu* 75 (2006), pp. 325–60.

4. On Laínez, see *Diego Laínez (1512–1565) and his Generalate: Jesuit with Jewish roots, close confidant of Ignatius of Loyola, preeminent theologian of the Council of Trent*, ed. Paul Oberholzer, S.J. (Rome: Institutum Historicum Societatis Iesu, 2015).

5. *Fontes narrativi*, vol. 1, p. 76. This letter is considered the first biographical sketch of Ignatius.

6. *Fontes narrativi*, vol. 1, p. 154.

7. *Fontes documentales de S. Ignatio de Loyola* (Rome: Institutum Historicum Societatis Iesu, 1977), p. 239.

8. *Saint Ignatius's Own Story*, p. 4 num. 2.

9. Jerónimo Nadal, a brilliant exegete, originally from Palma de Majorca, met Ignatius in Paris when they were pursuing their respective studies. He entered the Society in 1545 and held important functions within it: General Commissioner for Spain, Vicar General for the whole Society. He is one of the best exponents of the spirituality of Ignatius. On Nadal, see William V. Bangert, S.J., *Jerome Nadal, S.J., 1507–1580: Tracking the First Generation of Jesuits*, ed. Thomas M. McCoog, S.J. (Chicago: Loyola University Press, 1992).

10. Francisco de Borja, Marquis of Llombai, Viceroy of Catalonia, Duke of Gandía, a friend of King Charles I of Spain (later Holy Roman Emperor Charles V), was admitted into the Society after the death of his wife—at first secretly (1546), then publically (1550). After having exercised important functions in the Society, he was elected as the second successor to Ignatius (1565–1572) Some of his writings were condemned by the Inquisition because they believed they detected Lutheran tendencies in them. The most accessible biography is Cándido de Dalmases, S.J., *Francis Borgia: Grandee of Spain, Jesuit, Saint* (St. Louis: The Institute of Jesuit Sources, 1991). For a more detailed study see *Francisco de Borja y su tiempo: politica, religión y cultura en la Edad Moderna*, eds. Enrique García Hernán and María del Pilar Ryan (Valencia/Rome: Albatros Ediciones/Institutum Historicum Societatis Iesu, 2011).

11. *Fontes narrativi*, vol. 4, p. 9.

12. The "illuminated" or, in Spanish, *alumbrados,* refused any human mediation between God and his creatures. They were suspected of wanting to communicate directly with God, bypassing the authority of the Church and favoring personal meditations over vocal prayers, a cult of images, penitence and obedience. Those who succeeded at abandoning themselves to God (*dejados*) no longer had any need of merits and could no longer commit sin. See *Diccionario de espiritualidad ignaciana*, ed. José García de Castro, S.J. (2 vols., Bilbao: Mesajero/SalTerrae, 2007), vol.1, pp. 131–32.

13. A society of Jesuit scholars founded by the Belgian Jean Bolland (1596–1665) for the study of the lives and cult of the saints.

14. *Saint Ignatius's Own Story*, p. 7, num. 1.

15. *Fontes narrativi*, vol. 1, p. 156.

16. *Fontes narrativi*, vol. 2, p. 63.

II

THE GREAT REVERSAL

Once they had taken the city, the French, noble gentlemen that they were, took care of the wounded man, and "treated . . . [him] with great kindliness and courtesy."[1] Their doctors tried to reset the fractured leg and looked after him until he was well enough to be transported to Loyola, 12 to 15 days later. Once home, he took a turn for the worse and it was necessary to summon doctors and surgeons "from all parts to his bed."[2] Because the fracture had been badly set or, perhaps, the setting was undone during the journey, there was only one solution: a second operation to set the bones in place. This is what was done. Ignatius would remember it as "butchery" which he endured, as always, without saying a word, and simply by tightening his fists. In spite of everything, his overall state deteriorated to the point of manifesting symptoms indicative of an approaching death. On June 28, 1521, the doctors doubted that he would survive the night, and those near to him counseled him to go to confession and to receive the sacraments. It was the Vigil of the Feast of St. Peter—a saint to whom he had always been devoted. During the night, an improvement began: the sick man suddenly felt better and recovered his strength quite rapidly, to the point of seeming to be out of danger several days later. Whereas Ignatius, in his autobiographical narrative, speaks very soberly of the feast of the apostle to whom he attributed his healing, Ribadeneira wrote of an apparition of the saint "assisting him and nursing him to health."[3]

The resetting of the fracture, unfortunately, was not a success. The bones overlapped, forming an ugly growth beneath the knee. Henceforth he would not be able to wear the well-fitted and elegant boots of which he was so fond.

One leg was now shorter than the other, a handicap which his vanity found difficult to accept. He demanded that this outgrowth be removed in spite of all the pain which this new operation, without anesthesia, would involve. There was still the problem of trying to lengthen the leg using ointments and painful extensions which tortured him for many days. In spite of all this, he would still have a bit of a limp.

Although he was in good health, Íñigo was still unable to stand. Since he liked novels of chivalry, he asked for something to occupy his hours of convalescence. The library of the house was better stocked with edifying books than romantic novels. Magdalena, his sister-in-law, procured two books for him which she had brought back after a stay at the court; one was a Castilian edition of the *Vita Christi* by Ludolph of Saxony—also known as "the Carthusian" (d. 1378)[4]—and a life of the saints, the *Legenda aurea* or the *Flos sanctorum* by the Dominican Jacques de Voragine (d. 1298), two classics which nourished the popular piety of the Middle Ages.[5] The *Vita Christi* recounted the life and teachings of Jesus of Nazareth through a harmonization of the four Gospels, matched up with prayers, pious exercises, exhortations, and recommendations for the spiritual life. This would be Íñigo's first contact with the Word of God. The *Legenda aurae* proposed a journey through the liturgical year in the company of the saints with a marked emphasis on the heroic and marvelous aspects of their lives. As he read, new images gradually colonized his imagination as they intermingled with memories of his past life. Always present, almost invasive, the woman of his dreams seemed to occupy all his attention.[6] Like *Amadis of Gaul* and the knights with whom he still identified, he dreamed of rejoining her wherever she might be, to serve her, to write poems for her, to converse with her, and to accomplish many exploits in honor of her. These thoughts occupied his mind for hours. But the proud soldier was also fascinated by the heroism of the saints: "St. Dominic did this, therefore, I must do it. St. Francis did this; therefore, I must do it."[7] Even if that involved difficult and painful efforts, he considered himself up to it. These thoughts occupied his mind for long periods, and alternated with the worldly exploits which had always enthused him. At this stage it would be difficult to speak of conversion. Whether it was for God, for the king, or for the beautiful eyes of a woman, Íñigo remained the ambitious gentleman who only dreamt of gaining fame through courageous acts and a spirit of service. If the beneficiaries of his exploits changed, the motivation remained the same.

Íñigo, apparently gifted with a tremendous capacity for introspection, quickly realized that the memory of his maiden and his exploits at the court eventually tired him and left him "dry and dissatisfied."[8] On the other hand, the desire to imitate the austerities of the saints stimulated him and left him "cheerful and satisfied." Reflecting on the meaning of this, he gradually understood that different "spirits" were at work;[9] some stimulated and enlivened him; others made him withdraw into himself and left him sluggish and without enthusiasm. The change in the life of Íñigo was not as immediately striking as the French cannonball. He needed time to become a truly spiritual person: the long eight-month convalescence in the paternal mansion, then the wandering in the desert at Manresa, where, he said, the Lord treated him as a schoolmaster taught his students.[10]

Slowly, light entered his spirit; he began to reflect on his past life. If he was thinking about imitating the saints and the benefits of penance, he still had a superficial understanding of holiness. Generally he was more impressed by the spectacular austerity of his models than by their interior disposition. Like them, he wanted to go barefoot, eat only grass, subject himself to severe corporal penances, and practice all manner of austerities. But above all he wanted to go to Jerusalem "with all the disciplines and abstinences which a generous soul on fire with the love of God is wont to desire."[11] Little by little, these thoughts and the desires they nourished, banished memories of his past into the background until finally a spiritual experience confirmed his new orientation:

> One night, as he lay awake, he saw clearly the likeness of our Lady with the holy Child Jesus, at the sight of which he received most abundant consolation for a considerable period of time. He felt so great a disgust with his

past life, especially with its offenses of the flesh, that he thought all such images which had formerly occupied his mind were wiped out. And from that hour until August of 1553, when this is being written, he never again consented to the least suggestion of the flesh.[12]

So here he was, entirely taken up by the things of God. He continued to read during his convalescence even after he was able to move around the house. Anxious to edify, he spoke of his conversion to those around him. The interior transformation so manifested itself that his brother and the whole household understood that Íñigo had changed. An excellent calligrapher, he began to recopy the words of Christ in red ink and those of Mary in blue ink into a big notebook of 300 pages in quarto. This activity occupied a good part of his time. He devoted the rest of the time to prayer. He often spent a considerable amount of time in the contemplation of heaven and the stars "because when doing so he felt within himself a powerful urge to be serving our Lord."[13] He was impatient to be completely rehabilitated and only dreamt of setting out for Jerusalem.

And after Jerusalem? He would enter the Carthusian monastery in Seville, live there *incognito*, and follow a strict vegetarian diet. But, on second thought, it might be that the Carthusians would not let him indulge "the hatred he had conceived against himself" by practicing all the acts of penitence he wanted. But that was for later on! For the moment, he was only occupied with the voyage to the Holy Land. After 8 months of convalescence, when he had more or less recovered from his wounds, he announced to those near him that he was going to Navarrete to return to his place in the court of the Duke of Nájera. Martín, who was not taken in and who suspected some sort of irrational project, did all he could to hold him back. It was in vain! Without lying, but without telling the complete truth, Íñigo "slip[ped] away from his brother."[14]

Notes

1. *Saint Ignatius's Own Story*, p. 7, num. 2.

2. *Saint Ignatius's Own Story*, p. 7, num. 2.

3. *Life of Ignatius of Loyola*, p. 13.

4. See *La vida de Cristo: fielmente recogida del Evangelio y de los Santos Padres y doctores de la Iglesia*, ed. Emilio del Rio, S.J. (2 vols., Madrid/Rome: Universidad Pontificia de Comillas/Institutum Historicum Societatie Iesu, 2010).

5. For a new edition, see *Leyenda de los santos: (que vulgarmente Flos Santorum llaman): agora de nuevo empremida, y con gran estudio y diligencia extendida y declarada, y a la perfeción de la verdad traýda, y aún de las siguientes leyendas aumentada*, ed. Félix Juan Cabasés, S.J. (Madrid/Rome: Universidad Pontificia Comillas/Institutum Historicum Societatis Iesu, 2007). An English translation can be found in *The Golden Legend: Readings on the Saints*, ed. William Granger Ryan (2 vols., Princeton: Princeton University Press, 1995). See also Elizabeth Rhodes, "Ignatius, Women, and the *Leyenda de los santos*," in Maryks, *Companion*, pp. 7–23.

6. Unless she existed only in his fantasies, this mysterious lady—who, in his own words, was "neither countess, nor duchess, but of a nobility much higher" (*Saint Ignatius's Own Story*, p. 9, num. 6)—has been identified variously as Germaine of Foix, Leonor, a sister of Emperor Charles V, or, more probably, his youngest sister Catalina.

7. *Saint Ignatius's Own Story*, p. 10, num. 7.

8. *Saint Ignatius's Own Story*, p. 10, num. 8.

9. During the times of Ignatius, the word "spirit" is used to signify anything which causes a movement, which gives momentum, such as the wind and breath (*spiritus*). "Spirits can signify either the spiritual movements of the soul or the spiritual substances which produce these emotions. Both can be found in St. Paul (I Cor. 12) and St. John (I John 4)" (Francisco Suarez S.J., *De religione*, l. IX, c. 5, n. 41).

10. *Saint Ignatius's Own Story*, p. 22, num. 27.

11. *Saint Ignatius's Own Story*, p. 11, num. 9.

12. *Saint Ignatius's Own Story*, p. 11, num. 10.

13. *Saint Ignatius's Own Story*, pp. 11–12, num. 11.

14. *Saint Ignatius's Own Story*, p. 12, num. 12.

III

The Pilgrim

With only the liturgical hours of the Virgin, a pen case, and his famous 300 page notebook, Íñigo set forth, accompanied by a brother, doubtlessly Pedro, the future rector of the parish of Azpeitia, and two servants. At his request, the little group stopped off at the sanctuary of Our Lady of Aránzazu for a prayer vigil. There Íñigo hoped to draw strength for the journey. There too he made the vow of chastity to which Laínez refers: "And since he was more afraid of being vanquished in things related to chastity than in any other domain, he made a vow of chastity during the voyage and he made it to Our Lady for whom he had a particular devotion."[1] Then, after leaving his brother at their sister's house in Oñate, he continued on to Navarrete where, he pretended, he hoped to see the Duke of Nájera and collect back pay.

The duke was absent from Navarrete. His treasurer claimed that, due to lack of funds, the duke could not pay off the debt. Once the duke had been informed of this, he declared that despite his financial short-fall and the tightening of his purse strings, he had the money to pay Loyola. In fact, the duke offered him a post managing one of his properties. Moreover Íñigo was not asking for so much. Once he had recovered his money, he gave some to "certain persons to whom he felt some obligation" but without naming them.[2] The rest he donated towards the restoration and maintenance of a statue of the Virgin. After having dismissed his two servants who had accompanied him and definitively turning his back to his past, he mounted his mule and set off to Montserrat alone.

LIKE DON QUIXOTE

Alone on his mule, in pursuit of new adventures that would begin once he had been dubbed a knight, Íñigo has been interpreted by some as a Don Quixote of spirituality. But Ignatius of Loyola and Don Quixote were neither contemporaries nor co-nationals. The "Knight of the Woeful Countenance" was born 49 years after the death of Ignatius.[3] One is Castilian; the other, Basque. An enormous difference! If we are to believe Miguel de Unamuno, only one thing connected the two persons: a copy of Ribadeneira's biography of Loyola was among the books in the library of Don Quixote.[4]

Yet the comparison between Ignatius and Don Quixote is not as arbitrary as it might seem at first sight. Their respective itineraries traced a rite of initiation, of passage, through a series of analogous episodes and adventures, but their destination was very different. Each generous hero exemplified a particular conception of the human adventure: a desire to have a career, to serve, and to merit a glorious reputation. The same passion inspired their journey; both read avidly romances of chivalry, and, remarkably, *Amadis of Gaul*. Something led each to reorientate his life at a mature age. Íñigo was 31 and Don Quixote 50 when they left their homes after changing their names: Alonso Quijano will henceforth be called Don Quixote of La Mancha and Íñigo woull call himself "the Pilgrim." The first departure of Don Quixote, in secret, by the back door of the farmyard so as to escape the vigilance of a niece who served as his governess, recalls that of Íñigo shaking off his brother who was trying to dissuade him from his project. Don Quixote went forth into the world dreaming of the exploits he would accomplish, exploits that would later be celebrated by wise men; Íñigo departed for Montserrat alone with the intention of accomplishing "great, external works for so had acted the saints for God's glory."[5]

Like Íñigo, Don Quixote allowed the animal he was riding to determine his destiny; he departed "taking the road his horse chose, believing that was what the spirit of adventure called for."[6] Both wanted to go out into the world without money: one wanted to be received as a wandering knight without charge in the chateaux where he would be welcomed as a benefactor of humanity; the other desired God to be his only refuge. Fully confident in his destiny as a wandering knight, Don Quixote did not hesitate to board a boat without a tackle in order to let himself be carried by the flow of the water to liberate a princess imprisoned in a castle (Book II, c. 29); similarly Íñigo was ready, if the pope ever asked him, to board a ship in the port of Ostia without a mast, sails, oars, or food for a long voyage.

If knightly vigils, ideal and chaste relations with women, scorn of money, retreat into solitary places to do penance, visions in a cave at Manresa or in a grotto at Montesinos seem to draw them together, they were different. Don Quixote, in his contemplation, had no object other than his own dreams which he confused with reality. Enclosed within himself, he could only become delirious. When Íñigo had visions, what mattered to him were the effects which the mystical experience had on him and a means by which he could evaluate their authenticity. Don Quixote was a dreamer who inhabited an enchanted world. Reading romances introduced him to an imaginary world which he confused with reality. He exemplified goodness becoming a generosity without discernment. As dream replaced reality, he lived in a world of pure, immobile, beautiful, and incorruptible ideas. He became first comical then tragic. Like Quixote, Íñigo ran a very real risk of going astray when he aspired to serve Christ through a career of a wandering knight or a saint in order to attract the attention of the heavenly court. But he understood the potential for temptation and that every commitment to an ideal should, without exception, be an object of discernment and that every "spirit" should be authenticated by reality.

A NaÏve Zeal

The new life began with a departure, a journey. Íñigo left the family house for a pilgrimage to Jerusalem where he intended literally to walk in the footsteps of Christ. From this point on, he was a man on the move. In the depths of his heart, he sensed a call from above that impelled him to continue his journey towards something new. He was motivated by a greater service to the Lord. Íñigo accepted with courage and confidence things which bothered and frightened those around him. Since he felt that this impetus enlivened him and filled him with an interior peace and joy, he concluded that it came from God. Free of everything, unburdened, confiding solely in God's help, fearless, prudent, reflective, analytic, conscious of his strengths but without allowing any difficulty to deter him, the Pilgrim advanced, ready to go beyond new frontiers in order to respond to God's call as discerned through the ordinary circumstances of his life.

The road traveled was comprised of generous deeds. Every evening after his departure from Loyola, he subjected himself to corporal punishment (took the discipline). The austerities of the saints, which fascinated him more than their interior spirituality, easily reenforced his excessive and abso-lutist temperament. As if holiness could be obtained by the degree of auster-ity! Saint Humphrey, the extravagant anchorite of Thebaidan Egypt, seemed to be more important than the Gospel.[7] An incident during the journey indicated this shortsightedness. A Moor, with whom Íñigo was conversing, gladly admitted that Mary had conceived without male intervention, but, despite the Pilgrim's good arguments, he would not agree that she retained her virginity in childbirth. After having traveled together for a while, they parted. The Pilgrim, upset that he had not defended Mary's virginity better, decided to stab the Moor to honor the Virgin. He hesitated; he pondered both options; he became restless because he was unsure what he should do. He finally left the decision to his mule. He let go of the reins. If at the next fork in the road, the mule followed the Moor's path, the Pilgrim interpreted this as a sign that God wanted him to stab the Moor. If the mule horse took another path, the Moor would be spared. The Moor got lucky. When he dictated this story, Ignatius dwelt on it at length because he wanted it to make it understood how shortsighted he was at that time in spite of his great desires to serve the Lord.[8]

Somewhere before Montserrat, at Lleida (Lérida) or Igualada, the Pilgrim bought "some sacking of a very loose weave and a rough prickly surface" in order to make the vestment he had decided to wear to go to Jerusalem—a sort of robe which extended to his feet. A pilgrim's staff and a gourd completed the wardrobe of the perfect Pilgrim.[9] Because of his bad leg, he also bought a pair of espadrilles, but he only wore one on his injured foot.

So as to imitate better the legendary knights—whose stories still occupied much of his imagination—the Pilgrim decided to make a knightly vigil at the feet of the black Virgin of Montserrat. His preparatory general confession to Jean Chanon took three days. After the confession the Pilgrim handed his sword and dagger to Chanon for suspension at the altar of Our Lady, and gave his mule to the monastery. By night, in secret, he gave his gentleman's clothing to a poor man, and put on his new vestments; then, like Esplandián in the fourth book of *Amadis,* he spent the whole night "without either sitting or lying down, but standing a while and then kneeling, before the altar of our Lady of Montserrat where he had made up his mind . . . to clothe himself with the armor of Christ."[10] This was the night of March 24–25, 1522. Laínez attributed this vigil to the Pilgrim's ignorance of spiritual things, apparently inspired more by what he had read than by an authentic spiritual motivation, but Laínez quickly added that the Lord leads each according to his or her capacities and preferences.[11]

In order to escape notice, Íñigo did not take the road to Barcelona, a port of embarkation for the Holy Land, but made a detour towards Manresa where he hoped to spend a few days in a hospice to reflect on what had happened and to record "certain things" in his famous notebook. Had he not eradicated all signs of his social origin when he gave his clothes to a poor man? He wanted to free himself from a past to which he had definitively turned his back. But his generosity risked compromising his good intentions. The poor man to whom he had given his vestments was accused of having stolen them. When the officers caught up with Íñigo on the road to ask him if what that poor devil was contending was exact, Íñigo was obliged to tell the truth. Aware of his clumsiness and feeling sorry for the poor man whom he had embarrassed, he wept, according to Laínez, for the first time since his departure from Loyola.[12] It did not take much to encourage people to circulate edifying stories about him. These accounts were spread widely, exaggerated his merits, and seriously threatened the anonymity he so desired. He had no recourse but to hide his name and his origin.

NOTES

1. *Fontes narrativi*, vol. 1, pp. 74–76.

2. *Saint Ignatius's Own Story*, p. 13, num. 13.

3. The first part of the novel by Miguel de Cervantes dates from the beginning of January, 1605.

4. Unamuno, *Our Lord Don Quixote*, p. 32. Cervantes, however, had been a student at a Jesuit college. See Frédéric Conrod, "The *Spiritual Exercises* from Ignatian Imagination to Secular Literature," in Maryks, *Companion*, pp. 266–81.

5. *Saint Ignatius's Own Story*, p. 14, num. 14.

6. Miguel de Cervantes, *Don Quixote*, trans. Tom Lathrop (New York: Penguin, 2001), p. 26.

7. According to his biographer, Paphnutius the Ascetic, Humphrey lived like a savage in a grotto, naked, clothed only with his natural pilosity and his long hair which he never cut. He lived on bread, dates and grass; he fasted and abstained for long periods of time. See Pedro de Leturia, S.J., *Estudios ignacianos* (2 vols., Rome: Institutum Historicum Societatis Iesu, 1957), vol. 1, pp. 97–111.

8. *Saint Ignatius's Own Story*, pp. 13–15, nums. 14–16.

9. *Saint Ignatius's Own Story*, p. 15, num. 16.

10. *Saint Ignatius's Own Story*, p. 15, num. 17.

11. *Fontes narrativi*, vol. 1, p. 76.

12. *Fontes narrativi*, vol. 1, p. 76.

IV

THE HARD SCHOOL OF MANRESA

At Manresa, Íñigo lodged with the poor and gave free rein to his austerities: rigorous abstinence from meat and wine except on Sundays, frequent fasts, a regime almost exclusively of bread and water, the discipline three times a day, and long, interminable hours of prayer. Since he had always been vain about his personal appearance, he was now obsessed by a certain rage against his body: he let his hair grow in total disorder, like Saint. Humphrey; he cut neither his fingernails nor toenails; he did not bathe. His burlap robe reeked and was full of vermin. He begged for his sustenance and redistributed to the poor whatever he received from pious rich ladies impressed by his austerity. It did not take long for his health to become seriously compromised. The physical aspect of a man once solid and robust, had changed completely. So much so that on a winter day, he found himself obliged to accept help from his female admirers when they found him sick and half dead in a hermitage of Our Lady. After less than a year the authorities ordered Íñigo to be transported to the house of a friend where he was treated attentively. The prospect of death did not depress him. Indeed he even rejoiced in it. Was he not "a holy man," as those around him insinuated? Frightened by this temptation of vainglory, he ceaselessly ruminated over his sins, and insisted that these pious women only speak of him as a sinner.[1] His account does not say whether they obeyed him, but one thing is certain: they convinced him to dress more warmly, wear a cloak, cover his head, and wear shoes.

At the beginning, this adjusted regime seemed to suit him; he was living "as an angel," according to Polanco, in peace, experiencing neither consolation nor desolation.[2] During this period, a type of hallucination initially reassured him, and he was saddened after its disappearance. Something similar to a very shiny serpent with seven or eight eyes appeared to him as many as six times a day.

After four months, discouragement began to set in. How was he going to continue this style of life for the next seventy years? Realizing that the temptation came from the scheming serpent, he challenged it: if you can promise me a single hour of life, I will abandon my regime. On another occasion, alone at the hospice, he began to regret his donation of his vestments to the pauper. Feeling that sadness was taking root, he rejoined the poor people, and recovered his calm. At bedtime spiritual consolations intensified to the point that he lost the few rare hours dedicated. This excessively zealous devotion, which was not satisfied with the time dedicated to it during the day, aroused his suspicions. Upon reflection, he concluded that the good spirit counseled him to sleep during the time set aside for that. Each time, the temptation was vanquished by the return of reality: the incertitude of the hour of death, the poor in flesh and blood. A need for sleep prevented him from going daydreaming. In the *Spiritual Exercises*, Ignatius would point out how the enemy of human nature would act on the imagination and how temptation always invited us to escape from reality.[3] In this way he eventually understood that he should not have any scruples regarding the abandonment of a life style that undermined his health and handicapped his desire to "help souls." Henceforth he would cut his hair and nails, and would take better care of his person in order to be able to deal with people.

Ignatius spent a little less than a year at Manresa—from March 25, 1522 to mid-February 1523. After four months characterized by excesses but during which he experienced peace and inner joy, a difficult period loomed. He remarked that between divine consolations and severe interior trials, the Lord was treating him like a schoolboy as he was teaching him. With no experience and knowledge of spiritual things, he had allowed himself to be guided by a sort of instinct. Slowly he was discovering the principles of the spiritual life. The school was tough, and the student was treated severely.

Because of his ignorance? Because of the coarseness of his spirit? Or because he did not have a spiritual director but nonetheless was determined to serve God? That mattered little. He passed through disconcerting alternations. Now arid and without any attraction for prayer and the sacraments, now exalted and fervent as if a leaden weight had been lifted from his shoulders, he asked himself with anguish: "What kind of new life is this that we are now beginning?"[4]

For months a terrible crisis of scruples pushed him to despair, almost to suicide. Had he confessed his sins sufficiently? Had he forgotten something? Had he expressed himself clearly enough? Had he been understood correctly? He could well run from one confessor to another who tried to reassure him but nothing worked, nothing freed him from his anxiety. Well aware that these scruples were harming him, he was nonetheless incapable of getting rid of them by himself. The example of a saint who, through fasting, had obtained a grace from God, suggested a final resort. Íñigo decided to abstain from all eating and drinking until God came to help him or until he found himself at the point of death. When his confessor learned of this, he ordered him to cease this senseless abstinence. Íñigo obeyed and found a bit of respite. Two days later, the infernal merry-go-round resumed. Disgusted with the life he was leading, he was on the point of giving up when the Lord "awaken[ed] him as it were from sleep."[5] Having decided against another return to his past, he suddenly found himself freed from scruples and strengthened by a great lesson. As long as he had aspired to be the artisan of his own holiness through a regiment of prayers, confessions and austerities, he remained inextricably entangled within his own limitations, constantly caught up in the specter of his condition as a sinner. The day when he decided to abandon himself to God, to shun preoccupation with his past, and to entrust himself to his mercy, he found peace.[6]

Notes

1. *Saint Ignatius's Own Story*, p. 24, num. 32.

2. *Fontes narrativi*, vol. 1, p. 159.

3. *The Spiritual Exercises of St.* Ignatius, trans. Louis J. Puhl, S.J. (Chicago: Loyola University Press, 1951), pp.141–42, 148, nums. 315, 332.

4. *Saint Ignatius's Own Story*, p. 18, num. 21.

5. *Saint Ignatius's Own Story*, p. 21, num. 25.

6. This experience of Ignatius calls to mind Martin Luther's meditation on the Epistle of the Romans 1:17 with the sudden realization after a prolonged spiritual crisis that God gratuitously grants salvation in Jesus Christ who alone justifies us and redeems us independently of our own works and achievements. This was the so-called *Turmerlebnis* (Tower Experience). Within the early Society Luther and Loyola were often juxtaposed: the latter reversed and corrected the damage done by the former. Similarities would have been ignored if not repudiated. For a contemporary, irenic presentation, see Philip Endean, S.J., "Ignatius in Lutheran light," *Thinking Faith*, July 29, 2011, http://www.thinkingfaith.org/articles/20110729_2.htm, accessed April 10, 2016.

V

THE SPIRITUAL EXERCISES

A legend has it that Ignatius of Loyola received the *Spiritual Exercises* from the hands of Our Lady at Manresa. An iconography more concerned with piety than historical accuracy, represented him in a grotto, writing the *Exercises* under the dictation of the Virgin or receiving it from her hands as Simon Stock, the thirteenth-century English Carmelite, had allegedly received the scapular.

The *Exercises* did not fall from heaven as by an enchantment. If we want to find a distant ancestry for them, it would be better to look at Montserrat and the *Book of Exercises for the Spiritual Life* by Father García Jiménez de Cisneros, O.S.B. (d. 1510). When Ignatius visited the famous Benedictine Abbey, his confessor probably spoke to him about it or loaned him a *compendium* for the usage of pilgrims. In the *Devotio Moderna*[1] by which the reformer was much influenced, he counsels the practice of prayer and the necessity of "exercising" it.

The *Exercises* are essentially the reflection of what Íñigo had lived. His first experience was a fluctuation, a spiritual alternation stimulated by the lives of the saints and memories of his past life. Attentive to these variations, while continuing to read the life of Christ, he discovered, little by little, that the will of God was not hidden somewhere up in the sky but was inscribed within him. He embarked on an interior pilgrimage, towards the arcane secrets of his being where the desire of God was mingled with contradictory sentiments, egoistical or basely materialistic. He understood that following of Christ consisted less in accomplishing great deeds so as to appear remarkable to God and people, and more in his fidelity to the inner desire. When his life flourished and he progressed in love and freedom, he felt more and more in harmony with Christ and his saints. As he grew in faith, hope and love, and as peace and joy dwelt in the depths of his heart, he concluded that he was on the right path. He retained this state of "consolation" as a positive indication of the divine will, the criteria which would henceforth enable him to resolve his doubts, to make decisions that he deemed just, and to verify the authenticity of his mystical experiences. On the other hand, the action of the evil spirit manifested itself when life grew stagnant, relationships became difficult, when the person became so wrapped up in himself in a narcissist manner and darkness and turmoil invaded the soul. Then a person became lazy, melancholic, separated from his/her Creator, without confidence or love. These were his first steps in the subtle art of spiritual discernment—an art of which he would become the undisputed master.

In accepting what is constructive and life-giving, in eliminating what destroys and imprisons, it is not only the encounter with God which is at stake but also the fulfillment of human existence since the two go hand in hand. There is no longer any need to go out from one's self to meet God. A person encounters God by ascertaining the better part of himself provided, however, that he liberates himself from everything which could distort his decision. To arrive at that, he must liberate himself from everything and abandon himself without reserve even to the point of renouncing a certain type of holiness which is overly spectacular. This is the price of peace and joy. As long as one remains a prisoner of the opinions of others and his own impulses, he may be generous, but God eludes him. When he succeeds in liberating himself from everything including himself, he will become capable of finding God in every situation. The *Exercises* mark out this road to liberty. Their title announces it without ambiguity: "Spiritual Exercises Which have as their purpose the conquest of self and the regulation of one's life in such a way that no decision is made under the influence of any inordinate attachment."[2]

From his experiences, Íñigo deduced some principles of divine pedagogy which could be of profit to others. Little by little, he kept improving these first drafts until he put on the finishing touches while at Paris. The result was a little manual, written in a very structured style,[3] more similar to an instruction leaflet than a treatise of spirituality, and destined for those who "give" the *Exercises* and accompany others in their search for God's will. Its influence in the sphere of spirituality is such that it has been numbered among the books which have changed history. It is said that Vladimir Lenin admired it. In the 19th century, the Protestant scholar Heinrich Böhmer qualified it as a "book of human destiny." The Austrian historian René Fülöp-Miller—who cannot be suspected of partiality towards the Jesuits—wrote: "There is, indeed, no other work of Catholic literature which, for historical effect, can be compared with Ignatius's little book."[4]

Right from the start, the *Exercises* were suspected of fostering Illuminism. The reproach came mainly from the Dominican theologians of Salamanca: Melchor Cano (d. 1560) and Tomás de Pedroche (d. 1565). Their fame, their competence, and their passionate criticism made them formidable. Cano did not miss an occasion to attack the *Exercises* from the pulpit, in the classroom, or in conversations, and even expressed publically his astonishment that Pope Paul III had approved them with *Pastoralis officii cura* in 1548. His catalogue of grievances was impressive: the priority given to personal inspiration; low esteem for religious life; teaching on indifference with more than a hint of illuminism;[5] a prudent waiting period for those who wish to take vows; "a real plague" Cano noted in the margin of a copy which Juan Martínez Siliceo (1486–1557), Archbishop of Toledo, had confided to his examination. For the angry theologian, the Jesuits were to Spain what Luther was to Germany: they played into the hands of the demon, they maintained misplaced familiarities with women and demonstrated laxity in admitting to the sacrament of penance. They were the authentic forerunners of the Anti-Christ.[6] Such excessive language did not help Cano's cause and his criticisms did not seem to have had much of an impact. They did, however, reinforce the prejudices of Archbishop Siliceo. Jealous of the privileges granted to the Jesuits by the pope, he did all that he could to limit their activities within his diocese.[7] Among other things, he reproached them for not respecting the law of the *purity of blood (limpieza de sangre)* by admitting new Christians to their numbers, i.e. Jewish converts.[8] He entrusted the presidency of a commission set up to examine the *Exercises* to Pedroche, a notorious adversary of mystics and *alumbrados*. In a report reeking of self-importance, the Dominican-President attacked Ignatius more directly: he reproached him for being an uncultured person, unable to write his *Exercises* in Latin, more disposed to follow his own interior experiences and the unction of the Spirit rather than books of theology—all indications which smelled of the *dejados* (the indifferent) and the *alumbrados* (the illuminated).

In truth, the *Exercises* exhibit some characteristics of the theories of the *alumbrados* above all in the manner in which Ignatius claimed that individuals may experience God immediately, without mediation. But the learned censor, who confused the *Exercises,* a practical manual, with a theological thesis, could not accept that. Ignatius, who was less troubled by these attacks than his companions, refused to defend the *Exercises:* from the moment the pope had approved them, their defense was the Church's task.[9]

NOTES

1. A spiritual movement which originated in Belgium at the end of the 14th century, which taught meditation, interiority, renouncement of the world, an affective piety, but everything with moderation. One of its representatives is Thomas à Kempis (1380–1471), the author of *The Imitation of Christ,* the bedside book of Ignatius. See R.R. Post, *The Modern Devotion. Confrontation with Reformation and Humanism* (Leiden, E.J. Brill, 1968); John Van Engen, *Sisters and Brothers of the Common Life. The Devotio Moderna and the World of the Later Middle Ages* (Philadelphia: University of Pennsylvania, 2008). For representative writings, see *Devotio Moderna: Basic Writings,* ed. John Van Engen (New York: Paulist Press, 1988). On the significance of the *Imitation of Christ,* see Maximilian von Habsburg, *Catholic and Protestant Translations of the* Imitatio Christi, *1425–1650 from Late Medieval Classic to Early Modern Bestseller* (Farnham: Ashgate, 2011).

2. *Spiritual Exercises,* p. 11, num. 21.

3. See Roland Barthes, *Sade, Fourier, Loyola,* trans. Richard Miller (New York: Farrar, Straus, and Giroux, 1976), pp. 41–56.

4. *The Power and Secret of the Jesuits* (New York: Viking Press, 1930), pp. 15–16.

5. See David Marno, "Attention and Indifference in Ignatius's *Spiritual Exercises*," in Maryks, *Companion*, pp. 232–47.

6. See John O'Malley, *The First Jesuits* (Cambridge, Ma.: Harvard University Press, 1993), pp. 292–93. See also Terence O'Reilly, "The Spiritual Exercises and Illuminism: Dominican Critics of the Early Society of Jesus," in *Ite inflammate omnia*, ed. Thomas M. McCoog, S.J. (Rome: Institutum Historicum Societatis Iesu, 2010), pp. 199–228, and Enrique Garcia Hernán, *Ignacio de Loyola* (Madrid: Taurus, 2013).

7. When confronted with the harassments of Siliceo, Ignatius simply noted that the archbishop was old and that the Society was young so it would survive him! See *Life of Ignatius*, pp. 287–88.

8. Unlike the Dominicans, the Society was more receptive towards these "New Christians." See Robert Aleksander Maryks, *The Jesuit Order as a Synagogue of Jews* (Leiden: Brill, 2009); "Ignatius of Loyola and the Converso Question," in Maryks, *Companion*, pp. 84–103; "Purity of Blood," *Oxford Bibliographies*, http://www.oxfordbibliographies.com/view/document/obo-9780195399301/obo-9780195399301-0101.xml (accessed April 11, 2016).

9. *Remembering Íñigo. Glimpses of the Life of Saint Ignatius of Loyola. The Memoriale of Luis Gonçalves da Câmara*, eds. Alexander Eagleston and Joseph A. Munitiz, S.J. (Leominster: Gracewing, 2004), p. 185, num. 321.

VI

Mystical Graces

Mystical graces followed the initial desolation and trial. Íñigo had already had his first mystical experience one night during his convalescence in Loyola when he clearly saw "an image of Our Lady with the Holy Child Jesus." At Manresa, he made a little catalogue of the graces he received.[1] First there were great illuminations on the Trinity which he saw in the form of three keys of an organ. This inspired such devotion in him that he wept, shed abundant tears, and talked about it enthusiastically to everyone. From that moment on, devotion to the Trinity would be one of the characteristics of his prayer. Although his formation was still very shaky and he only knew how to read and write, he started compiling what would become an eighty-page treatise on the Trinity! He received other lights on the way God created the world and how Christ is present in the Blessed Sacrament. Often, while he was at prayer, the humanity of Christ appeared to him in the form of a white body without detail. Ordinarily, with his interior eyes, he saw luminous images which, even though they were rather poor and hazy, enlightened him on the great mysteries of the faith: creation, the Trinity, and the Incarnation. These experiences and others later on had such a strong impact on his affectivity that they affected his body: abundant tears, sobs, body heat, exuberant and even visible joy. They were so strongly implanted in him that he imagined that if—impossibly—"there were no Scriptures to teach us these matters of faith, he was determined to die for them, merely because of what he had seen."[2]

Íñigo did not bother to describe these visions nor analyze them in detail. He preferred instead to examine the effects they produced in his soul. Do they leave him consoled, free on a long-term basis, in peace, full of inner joy, with an increase of faith, hope and love, confirmed in his desire to serve and to love? If so, he concluded, they come from God.

One experience left a special mark on him: an "illumination" rather than a vision, which came to him during a walk along the banks of the Cardoner, a river near Manresa. When he sat down for a moment to meditate, while still looking at the river down below, "the eyes of his understanding began to open. He beheld no vision, but he saw and understood many things, spiritual as well as those concerning faith and learning. This took place with so great an illumination that these things appeared to be something altogether new."³ Íñigo grasped, in their totality, the mysteries of the faith, the realities of the world and of history.

What happened? As was his custom, Ignatius did not describe the mystical event himself; he spoke more of its fruits: According to Laínez, "he had a new way of looking at things, the knowledge of many things both spiritual things known through faith and things of profane culture." Nadal added that the enlightenment he received did not concern just the mysteries of the faith but also the essence of the world "as if he had seen the cause and origin of every-thing [. . . .] As if the foundation of all things had been revealed to him."⁴ From this moment on, he looked at everything differently.⁵ Later while he was drawing up the *Constitutions*, and he had to make decisions regarding specific points of the new order, Íñigo would evoke the experience at the Cardoner as a reference point indicating the direction to be taken.

In what did this new perspective consist? In a sort of architectural vision, Íñigo grasped spiritual and profane realities in one movement. He saw every-thing in God. Understanding that God is the Creator of nature as He is the Author of grace, Íñigo could no longer separate the two orders, doing away with the fissure between a world here below, the world of humans, and a world above, the world of God, the division between the sacred and the profane. Henceforth, every creature, every situation, every circumstance could be the occasion for adoration and service: "*En todo amar y servir*" ("in all things [to]

love and serve the Divine Majesty").[6] Nadal summarized the essential fruit
of his vision "find[ing] God in all things."[7] This is why, in the *Constitutions,*
Íñigo gave considerable importance not only to the spiritual virtues, but also
to natural virtues and human qualities.

Henceforth the intuition of Cardoner would act as the principle and the
foundation of all his undertakings. Ignatius did not study theology; he lived
a formative mystical experience. During a period in which society's paradigm
was shifting as it passed from a medieval concept marked by Scholasticism to a
model inspired by the Renaissance, Íñigo proposed a new anthropological and
theological synthesis in which the person assumed the status of a responsible
subject, autonomous and free, capable of finding the will of God inscribed
within, and not somewhere up in the clouds above and beyond. This vision
of God and the world belied a reproach that he remained a prisoner of the
Middle Ages without daring to make a step towards the Renaissance.[8]

The illumination lasted some time. On his knees, at the feet of a cross,
Íñigo thanked God. Then the vision that had haunted him before—the serpent
with many of eyes—appeared again but less brilliant. For the first time he
clearly identified it; he was convinced that it was a demon. He chased it with
a club. The vision would continue to haunt him in Paris and in Rome, but,
according to Polanco, it had lost its seductive power.[9]

TEARS AND SOBS

The phenomena linked to mystical graces accompanied Ignatius throughout
his life. If, during his stay in Paris, his studies relegated them to the background, they reappeared with force at Venice and at Vicenza, on the road to
Rome, and again while he was working on the *Constitutions.* Visions, illuminations, interior voices, consolations without cause, raptures, physical reactions,
sobs and tears, all occupied a great part of his spiritual life. Above all, the
tears which he shed up to six or seven times a day, during prayer, reading the
breviary, or celebrating the Eucharist predominated to the point of putting his

life in danger. The doctor forbade him to weep, and his companions obtained for him a dispensation from the breviary as a precaution.[10]

These tears were a sign of the consolation that filled his heart, the bodily echo of the happiness of feeling empowered and carried by the presence of the Trinity. Although such phenomena were not rare in mystics, their frequency and intensity in Ignatius are especially noteworthy. As if they were the barometer of his spiritual life, he mentioned tears 175 times in his writings, especially in his *Spiritual Journey* (158 times between February 2 and March 12, 1544!). During the last nine months, he practically noted nothing else. They were a sign of a good spirit and of the proximity of God, whereas the evil spirit inspired dryness and not tears. If he attached considerable importance to tears—to the point of worrying when they do not come to ratify a decision—he was still wary of them. Being consulted about such things, he replied that one should not ask for the gift of tears in an absolute way because the gift was not necessary and not always good for everyone. In 1553, he wrote that weeping did not mean that someone was more charitable or better than others.[11]

Íñigo loved to contemplate nature—plants, insects, even worms. Everything spoke to him of God. The star-filled sky transported him. During his convalescence at Loyola, the contemplation of the sky and the stars enflamed him with a desire to serve the Lord. Laínez relates that years later, in Rome, Íñigo ascended to the terrace where he could see the heavens, took off his biretta, and remained standing there with eyes lifted towards the sky. He then prostrated himself. As years went by, as he became weak, he would sit on a little bench and remain there, immobile, with head bared, weeping in silence, so softly that no one heard his sobs and groans.[12]

Ignatius of Loyola does not have a reputation of being a mystic. Public opinion sees him more as a man of action, an apostle, an ascetic or a strategist of the apostolate, but does not rank him alongside a Francis of Assisi (1182–1226), a Teresa of Ávila (1515–1582), or a John of the Cross (1542–1591). He has not left any mystical writings; only a few surviving sheets of his *Spiritual Journal,* which he had hastened to destroy, bear witness to the mystical experiences which accompanied him as he wrote the *Constitutions.* The *Spiritual Exercises* are more a manual for action than a mystical treatise. Although they seem to lift the barricade between God and the soul by inviting the retreatant to speak with God "as a friend talks to a friend," they do not invite the retreatant to live a sort of nuptial union, but rather suggest a mysticism of service and commitment.[13] Ignatius was capable of finding God at the very heart of his activity at any hour; he was united to God like a docile instrument in the hands of the user.[14] When he contemplated the Divine Persons, he saw them acting for the salvation of the world.[15] Also, for him, the apostolic project determined his union with God, and he remained suspicious of anyone who attached too much importance to fusional pseudo-mystical phenomena such as the young Portuguese Jesuits to whom he wrote:

> They can practice seeking the presence of the Lord in all things; for example, in conversing with someone, in coming and going, in looking at things, in tasting things, in listening,—in brief in all our actions, because it is true that His Divine Majesty is in all things by His Presence, His Power and His Essence. This form of meditation which consists in finding God in all things, is easier than lifting one's self up into the more abstract Divine Mysteries if the person makes a great effort to render himself present. This excellent exercise will dispose us to receive the great visitations of the Lord, even during a brief prayer.[16]

NOTES

1. *Saint Ignatius's Own Story*, pp. 22–24, nums. 28–31.
2. *Saint Ignatius's Own Story*, p. 23, num. 29
3. *Saint Ignatius's Own Story*, p. 24, num. 30.
4. *Fontes narrativi*, vol. 2, p. 240.
5. *Fontes narrativi*, vol. 1, pp. 80–85.
6. *Spiritual Exercises*, p. 101, num. 233.
7. *Epistolae P. Hieronymi Nadal Societatis Iesu ab anno 1546 ad 1577 (5 vols.,* Madrid/Rome: Lopez del Horno/ Institutum Historicum Societatis Iesu, 1898–1962), vol. 4, p. 651.

8. Cf. Jorge Oteiza, as quoted by Ignacio Cacho Nazabal, S.J., *Ignacio de Loyola, ese enigma* (Bilbao: Mensajero, 2003), p. 342.

9. *Fontes narrativi*, vol. 1, p. 160.

10. *Remembering Íñigo*, pp. 109–10, nums. 180, 183.

11. Ignatius to Nicholas De Gouda, S.J., Rome, November 22, 1553, in *Letters and Instructions*, eds. Martin E. Palmer, S.J., John W. Padberg, S.J., and John L. McCarthy, S.J. (St. Louis: The Institute of Jesuit Sources, 2006), pp. 449–50.

12. *Life of Ignatius*, pp. 345–47.

13. For Gottfried Maron, the practice of the "colloquy" with the Lord proposed in the *Exercises* is a novelty in religious literature. See *Ignatius von Loyola: Mystik, Theologie, Kirche* (Göttingen: Vandenhoeck & Ruprecht, 2001), pp. 76–77.

14. *Saint Ignatius's Own Story*, pp. 69–70, num. 99.

15. *Spiritual Exercises*, p. 49, num. 102.

16. Loyola to Antonio Brandao, Rome, June 1, 1551, *Letters and Instructions*, pp. 339–45.

VII

The Pilgrim on

the Psychiatrist's Couch

Speculating on the whole career of Ignatius, William W. Meissner[1] interpreted the behavior of the young *hidalgo* (nobleman) as an indication of a phallic narcissism animated by a powerful libido. His need to be admired, his comportment towards women, his aggressive haughtiness, his authoritarianism were all signs of this. The absence of a mother during his tender years, the strong and virile image of his father, his education at the court partially explained this. When this ideal collapsed as the result of a cannonball, he underwent a profound crisis; the breakdown of his narcissist self, shattered his very identity. The discovery of the saints and the reading of the life of Christ enabled him to begin its reconstruction around a new ideal: the total handing over of his life to God's will and a commitment without reserve to the service of Christ. But time and struggles were necessary for him to arrive at the reorientation of his narcissism and his libido. The need to be admired is not death nor a need to seduce. By imitating the saints, the new convert persisted in wanting to have a career, and be noticed. A victim of a tendency towards scrupulosity and a morbid sentiment of guilt, he directed his aggressiveness against himself through excessive acts of penitence. A masochistic contempt of himself took him to the brink of suicide. During his stay at Manresa certain repressive behaviors bordered on hysteria.

Once he had hit rock bottom with the destruction of his first ideal, Ignatius undertook an astonishing spiritual ascension during which the self reintegrated. After the destructive process which almost led to the dissolution of the *hidalgo*'s personality, another process, this time constructive, began and from this would emerge the saint, the founder, and animator of an original religious order. In a bitter struggle, ascetic battles alternated with phases of regression. An explanation of this evolution can be found in what the psychoanalyst calls a "transvaluation" of primitive impulses: the ideal of youth ceded place to a new ideal founded on spiritual values and animated by extremely religious ambitions exemplified by the saints and, above all, by Christ. The aggressive, libidinous, narcissist energies of his youth, frustrated by the accident and the ensuing illness, were not abolished but rather reinvested in the service of the "will of God" through a dramatic confrontation between self and Superego. The values which formerly motivated him become internalized; the ideal of self was modified with the complicity of the Superego, but remained animated by the legacy of his youth and fiercely resistant, since the image of the phallic, powerful and domineering father, and the influence of an absent mother perceived as passive, vulnerable, religious and idealized, still dwelt within him.

By the means of this dynamic, grace impelled Íñigo towards Christ, carrying his cross. Insofar as he identified himself with Christ, the narcissist desire of heroism succeeded. Henceforth, he could become a hero of God like the saints he admired. Following Christ who was poor and humiliated disarmed his aggressiveness and calmed his libido. To be sure, he would retain these characteristics. His insistence on obedience and his authoritarian manner would be a reflection of his own problems with obedience; his comportment with women would fluctuate between the need for a substitute mother and the need to seduce; his insistence on the examination of conscience might well be a sign of an obsessive character. This would not prevent the self and the Superego from becoming integrated over time. When Ignatius speaks of his itinerary as a pilgrimage, he is not speaking in vain.

In the face of the impulses of his psyche, he kept control over his person and remained the master of what he did. On the other hand, he always functioned as a well-informed chief, a spiritual director full of wisdom, and a practical organizer; in a word, as a realistic and objective person. Far from being a dreamer or a psychopath, Ignatius was fundamentally reasonable. Meissner notes:

> . . . if a modern psychiatrist had had the opportunity to examine Íñigo de Loyola during the period of post conversion turmoil and the severe crisis at Manresa, he might have diagnosed him as psychotic, possibly with quali-fications. [. . .] If that same psychiatrist had the opportunity to consult the patient again in his later years, when he was General of the Society of Jesus, governing its world-wide operations and complex and difficult relations with royalty and the papal court, he might have formed a different impres-sion. Certainly he would hardly have thought of psychosis, but would more likely have been impressed, as so many of Ignatius' contemporaries were, by the composure and power of this extraordinary man.[2]

NOTES

1. *Ignatius of Loyola. The Psychology of a Saint* (New Haven: Yale University Press, 1992). The author was a Jesuit, a doctor in medicine and psychoanalysis. He taught at Boston College and prac-ticed analysis at the Psychanalytic Insti-tute of Boston.

2. Meissner, *Ignatius of Loyola*, p. 328.

VIII

Jerusalem, the Shattered Ideal

A Turbulent Voyage

Around the middle of February 1523, Iñigo left Manresa for Barcelona where he hoped to find a ship bound for Jerusalem. Other people who were traveling the same route proposed that they journey together. Even though he had no language skills, Iñigo preferred to go his own way, since he had decided against any refuge and to rely on God alone: "If he had a companion he would expect help from him when he was hungry. And would thus trust in him, and be drawn to place his affection in him, when he wanted to place all his confidence and affection and hope in God alone."[1] Pushing confidence to the extreme, he even intended to embark without provisions—something which did not please the captain of the boat. The captain was willing to accept him aboard without charging him, but he was not going to allow him to leave without food for the journey. This caused a serious problem of conscience: how could one pretend to put all confidence in God and yet look for provisions? Perplexed, he left the decision to his confessor who advised him to take enough victuals for the crossing. Twenty days later, he set sail for Italy after leaving a few extra sous from his begging on a public bench. When people would ask him where he wanted to go, he did not dare say that he was leaving for Jerusalem through fear of vanity, which pursued him almost obsessively, to the point that he never dared to say what country he was from or to which family he belonged.

The crossing from Barcelona to Gaeta was rapid, but not at all restful because of a severe storm. Once they had landed, the dangers did not lessen.

Íñigo traveled with a woman and her daughter who was disguised as a boy to escape the covetousness of the males. They were forbidden to enter towns because of fear of the plague. Thus it was impossible for him to beg for his bread and to find an inn for the night. They found refuge in isolated farms which served as quarters for soldiers. Íñigo so ferociously defended the virtue of his traveling companions against these soldiers that everyone was terrified.

Exhausted by the crossing, by lack of food, and by the fatigues of the journey, Íñigo, at the end of his rope, stopped at Fondi for two days to rest and to beg what he needed until he got to Rome. He arrived there on Palm Sunday, March 29, 1523. He passed Holy Week and Easter at Rome, visiting the tombs of the Apostles, begging his subsistence, and obtaining authorization from Pope Adrian VI to travel to the Holy Land. All who knew about his project tried to dissuade him. No one could travel to Palestine without money. Indeed the attempt was foolish: no ship would accept him aboard. Thus he should abandon his dreams and be reasonable. Without budging, Íñigo placed his confidence in God. Nonetheless, he took a little money with him–six or seven ducats—as a prevision for the crossing—when he set out for Venice. Two days later, he regretted his lack of confidence and distributed his nest egg to the poor.

The road to Venice was complicated because of the plague. The cities were closed, and he had to sleep wherever he found a place. Pale and weak, his complexion turning yellow, a veritable walking corpse, Íñigo did not even have the strength to keep up with traveling companions. Soon left behind, alone, at night, just outside of Chioggia on the road to Padua, Christ appeared to him "as He was accustomed to"[2] to strengthen him. He set out again with renewed vigor, without even worrying about obtaining the indispensable certificate of good health. But this did not prevent him from entering and leaving Padua without being bothered by the guards.

At Venice, Providence awaited him. A rich Spanish fellow-citizen whom he met in his comings and goings in the city invited him to dine. As was his custom, Íñigo did not talk during the meal except to answer questions. He listened attentively to the conversations "and made note of some things from which he later took occasion to speak of God. When the meal was over this is what he did."[3] His host was very impressed and lodged him up to the moment of his departure. His host even set up an audience with the Doge Andrea Gritti, who obtained a free passage for him on the ship of the new governor of Cyprus. On July 14, 1523, without having fully recovered from a strong fever and against the advice of the doctor, Íñigo embarked on the *Negrona*. Because he protested vigorously against the homosexual practices that he had witnessed on the ship, the sailors resolved to abandon him on an island. A change in the winds frustrated this project.[4] They arrived within sight of Jaffa on August 25 but had to wait until August 31 to disembark because of the administrative harassments on the part of the Turkish authorities. On September 4, riding little donkeys, the pilgrims finally came within sight of Jerusalem where they were greeted by the Franciscans.[5]

To See the Traces of the Lord

Without elaboration Íñigo insisted on the fruits of his stay in Jerusalem. The life of the Lord, contemplated with devotion, took form in his imagination. In the *Exercises,* Ignatius counseled the retreatant to begin prayer by imagining the material setting of the scene he wants to contemplate so as to find his own place there, the so-called "composition of place."[6] At Jerusalem, Íñigo paid attention to all details in order to identify himself with Christ and walk in his footsteps. For him, sight played an essential role in the perception of the mystery. Once he wanted to call attention to himself in court; now as a new convert, he aspired to be seen by the Lord. By prioritizing "interior vision," Ignatius used the image as a new language about God. Roland Barthes noted that Íñigo thus situated himself fully in the modern epoch which gave priority to the eye as illustrated in the baroque style.[7] Throughout the Middle Ages until the 16th century, hearing was the privileged sense of perception, and the ecclesiastical hierarchy based its authority on "hearing" the Word. *Fides ex auditu*, faith comes from hearing, as St. Paul stressed in Romans 10:17.

Íñigo's intention evolved after his departure from Loyola. Whereas he had initially intended to go to Jerusalem to live a life of penitence, he now wanted to remain there to frequent the Holy Places and to "help souls." Confident in his letters of recommendation, he asked the Franciscan guardian for permission to reside in Jerusalem for devotional purposes—being careful not to mention his intention to help souls lest that be grounds for refusal. Unfortunately, this would hardly be possible: the convent was poor and had to support its actual members; moreover, pilgrims created too many difficulties for the Franciscans at their death or capture by the Turks because friars were expected to pay ransom. Íñigo was not worried: he had decided to remain despite the possible consequences. To combat Íñigo's stubbornness, the Franciscan superior resorted to extreme measures and even threatened him with excommunication. The warning was serious and, in the end, Íñigo complied. But before he left, he wanted to see again the rock on which Jesus was standing at the moment of the Ascension because "the print of His footstep is still to be seen."[8] It could be found in the ancient Church of the Ascension, converted into a mosque by Saladin in 1198. Secretly, without a guide, he set out towards the Mount of Olives. There he bribed the guards with a penknife and was able to enter the precinct. A moment later, not remembering in which direction Christ "was facing," he returned to the site and again bribed the guards with a pair of scissors. He was later severely reprimanded for this dangerous adventure. Although he was treated harshly by a guard from the convent who had been sent out to look for him, he was very consoled because "he thought he saw [the Lord] above him all along the way."[9]

New Horizons

Influenced by the reading of the *Vita Christi* by Ludolph of Saxony, Íñigo had wanted to live in the Holy Land to put his foot literally in Jesus' path.

Contemporary political events frustrated his plans and purified his desire without causing him to question the project itself. He was now forced to seek his Palestine elsewhere even if, several years later, the idea of living in the Holy Land returned, only to be thwarted once again. Reality and concrete circumstances compelled him to a more ample understanding of his vocation.

He was back in Italy, in the middle of winter, after an agitated crossing during which several ships lost their crews and cargo. At Venice, in the middle of January 1524, the same friends who had received him prior to his departure again came to his aid, giving him money and "a piece of fabric" so that he might protect himself from the cold. But an essential question still remained: now what? One thing was always certain: he wanted to "help souls."

Help souls! The idea had taken shape over the years. At the beginning of his conversion, Íñigo only thought of living for Christ, of doing penance in a Carthusian monastery, at Jerusalem, or in some solitary place where he could freely exercise "the hatred he had conceived against himself."[10] Little by little, through chance encounters, a desire to help others became more evident and transformed itself into a firm proposal when he was in Jerusalem.[11] This was a project not lacking in audacity for someone without any proper formation. Since he could not remain in Palestine, the most useful thing he could do so as to help others more efficaciously, would be to study. Thus he decided to return to Barcelona via Genoa.

The journey across Italy was no walk in the park as Charles V and the French King Francis I contested the duchy of Milan. Unburdened of his money by the beggars, without any means, obliged to fast once again, Íñigo traveled through regions infested with soldiers from both sides. Stopped several times by both the Spanish and the French, taken for a spy, stripped of his clothing, submitted to a humiliating search, led half naked through the streets, he hardly manifested any emotion. As when he was treated harshly in Jerusalem, a vision of Christ going to his Passion consoled him. During an interrogation by a captain, Íñigo's awkward manner of speaking, crude replies, and his voluntary lack of courtesy led the soldiers to take him for a madman "like Christ before Herod." Always concerned with walking in the footsteps of "his Lord," Íñigo, far from fleeing humiliations and opprobrium, sought them as the proof of a supreme fidelity. In the *Exercises,* at the moment when the retreatant prepares to make decisions which will influence the orientation of his life, Ignatius invites him to consider what he estimates to be the summit of love and humility:

> . . . in order to imitate and be in reality more like Christ our Lord, desire and choose poverty with Christ poor, rather than riches; insults with Christ loaded with them, rather than honors; I desire to be accounted as worthless and a fool for Christ, rather than to be esteemed as wise and prudent in this world.[12]

After many adventures, he finally arrived at Genoa. Providential encounters with Basques, both French and Spanish, one of whom had on different occasions spoken to Íñigo while he was in service to the Spanish king, helped him find a berth on a ship bound for Barcelona.

Notes

1. *Saint Ignatius's Own Story,* p. 26, num. 35.

2. *Saint Ignatius's Own Story,* p. 30, num. 41.

3. *Saint Ignatius's Own Story,* p. 31, num. 42.

4. *Life of Ignatius,* pp. 42–44.

5. A Swiss pilgrim, Peter Füssli of Zurich, kept a journal of the trip in the Swiss-German dialect. See Ricardo García-Villoslada, S.J., *San Ignacio de Loyola: nueva bibliografía* (Madrid: Biblioteca de Autores Cristianos, 1986), p. 244.

6. *Spiritual Exercises,* p. 25, num. 47.

7. Barthes, *Sade, Fourier, Loyola,* p. 65.

8. *Saint Ignatius's Own Story,* p. 34, num. 47.

9. *Saint Ignatius's Own Story,* p. 34, num. 47.

10. *Saint Ignatius's Own Story,* p. 12, num. 12.

11. This ideal will find its institutional expression in the foundation of the Society of Jesus: "The end of this Society is to devote itself with God's grace not only to the salvation of the members' own souls, but also with that same grace to labor strenuously in giving aid toward the salvation and perfection of the souls of their fellowmen" (*Constitutions,* pp. 77–78, num. [3]).

12. *Spiritual Exercises,* p. 69, num. 167.

IX

Tardy and Disrupted Studies

Barcelona: Grammar Studies

At Barcelona Íñigo found Isabel Roser, his benefactor who had facilitated his departure for Jerusalem. He also met a schoolmaster, Jerónimo Ardévol, who was teaching Latin grammar. Both approved of his project to study: Isabel would take care of his sustenance and Ardévol would give him free tuition. In fact, Íñigo begged for his food despite the consistent alms given by Isabel and her female friends. Thus a thirty-year old man repeated his lessons amidst children as he tried to learn declensions and rules of grammar by heart. This was a difficult undertaking for someone his age, all the more so because spiritual reflection and mystical experiences occupied so much of his time until he understood that God willed that he study and he solemnly promised his teacher that he would not miss another lesson. Once again, a return to reality liberated him.

While at Barcelona, as he pondered what he would do after his studies, he considered the possibility of entering a religious order—but not just any-where but "in a lax or scarcely reformed order" so that he could suffer more.[1] Meanwhile, he made an effort to restore religious discipline in the Dominican convent of Our Lady of the Angels whose nuns' behavior was causing scandal in the city. This initiative ended with Íñigo being seriously beaten up by a thug hired by the gallants who frequented the convent. He was left half-dead in the street. His friends, the Pascual family, took him in and he remained in bed for 53 days.

After two years, his academic progress was satisfactory enough for Master Ardévol and another doctor to advise him to follow the liberal arts course, the equivalent of philosophy courses, at Alcalá. Íñigo left an impression of a very engaging and spiritual person, harsh on himself but full of kindness towards others, impassioned for Christ, dedicated to helping souls, and preoccupied with religious reform. He also bid farewell to some very good friends to whom he would remain faithful: Isabel Roser whom he called his "second mother," the Pascual family, Sister Teresa Rejadella, and other persons with whom he would keep up a more or less consistent correspondence. Polanco reported that Íñigo also left behind three companions eager to share his life: Calisto de Sa and Lope de Cáceres of Segovia, and Juan de Arteaga of Estepa—a modest beginning of disciples.[2]

AT ALCALÁ: PHILOSOPHY

At Alcalá, Íñigo remained faithful to his style of life. He begged and lived only from alms even if that invited the ridicule of passersby. Once an ecclesiastic humiliated him in public and in a very ugly way. The director of the hospice of Our Lady of Mercy witnessed this incident, and offered Íñigo a room in his establishment and everything necessary for his sustenance: food, a bed, and a candle.

Íñigo stayed at Alcalá from March 1526 to June 1527.[3] There he made some acquaintances and won over some friends—among others, the brothers Diego and Miguel de Eguía who helped him with alms.[4] On the counsel of his confessor, Manuel Miona,[5] he began reading the *Enchiridion militis Christi* of Erasmus, edited in Castilian by his friends, the Eguías, a bestseller that delighted the partisans of Church reform. But the frigid style and acerb criticisms of the Dutch humanist did not appeal to his sensitivity and his concept of fidelity to Christ and his Church. Rather than feel himself confirmed in his desire for reform, his fervor cooled. He rather quickly gave up this reading, impressed by the warnings of preachers and other theologians critical of Erasmus. Later, he would formally advise against reading Erasmus, preferring the *Imitation of Christ* which, since Manresa, had become his bedside book.[6]

The courses in philosophy and theology were based on the *Sentences* of Peter Lombard (1100–1160), the *Physics* of Albert the Great (1193–1280), and the *Logical Terms* or *Summulae* of Domingo de Soto (1494–1560). This was one ambitious project! Too ambitious for the apostolic zeal which still occupied a good part of his time. Later on, Íñigo would confess that he had, in fact, studied very little at Alcalá and what he had learned was not very solid. He offered reasons for this: he was giving the spiritual exercises, teaching catechism, engaging in spiritual conversation, and counseling. So successful was he that passersby regularly gathered around him for instruction.

The three companions from Barcelona plus a young Frenchman, Juan de Reinalde, or "Juanico," rejoined him at Alcalá. Íñigo was delighted. They all dressed in the same way. Small groups of people, especially pious ladies, gathered in his room where Íñigo explained the catechism, taught them how to pray, to go to confession, to examine their conscience, and proposed other spiritual exercises.

A Person of Interest for the Inquisition

This activity did not pass unnoticed, all the more so in that some of these ladies had fainting spells. Throughout the city, rumors and comments about the "Iñiguistas" (Íñiguists) circulated widely. Should not these persons in soutanes be included among the "Illuminati"? Such suggestions were all that was required to arouse the interest of the Inquisition. Investigators from Toledo went over the life of Íñigo and his companions with a fine-tooth comb without discovering anything reprehensible. The Vicar General in charge of the case, Juan Rodríguez de Figueroa, simply asked that they no longer go around barefoot and that they not dress in the same way because they were not consecrated religious. So the clothes were dyed black and brown, and Íñigo wore shoes and everything returned to normal until, four months later, on March 6, 1527, a new inquiry was opened. The Inquisition had been informed that an upper-class, married woman visited Íñigo in his room at the hospice in the early morning. The case too was quickly closed, but that did not mean that the problems with the Inquisition were over.

A local policeman later arrested Íñigo. What was the charge? He promoted observance of the Sabbath—surely a sign that he was a *converso*—and had encouraged a woman and her "very young and very pretty" daughter to make a barefoot pilgrimage to the sanctuary of Saint Veronica in Jaén, a distance of 300 kilometers. Íñigo replied that he could not think of any better way to observe the Sabbath than by a particular devotion to Our Lady on that day. Moreover, around Alcalá there were no Jews. As for the ladies, he never encouraged them to embark on such an adventure. Nonetheless, he still had to wait patiently in jail for 42 days until the two women returned and verified his deposition. Putting all his confidence in God alone, Íñigo refused to be defended by a lawyer, and to let his well-placed friends intervene on his behalf: "He for Whose love I came here will release me when it seems good to Him."[7] Despite their exoneration, Íñigo and his companions were again condemned to dress like other students and, under pain of excommunication, forbidden to speak on matters of faith for four years until they had finished their studies.[8]

The investigations of the Inquisition and the judgment of Figueroa represent Íñigo's first contact with the ecclesiastical hierarchy. He submitted to its judgment without allowing himself to be overawed by the terrible tribunal. Placing himself entirely in God's hands, he confronted the investigators and judges with respect, to be sure, but also a disconcerting liberty. When Figueroa told him that he will be burnt at the stake if he were found guilty of any heresy, he replied: "They would burn you too, if they found you in heresy."[9] The vicar himself ended up buying them new clothes.

Although he was not at all troubled by these harassments, Íñigo, in spite of everything, tired of the restrictions. The prohibition to help souls, for no other reason than his lack of education, did not convince him at all. So he considered leaving Alcalá to continue his studies in Salamanca where his four companions had already preceded him. For his own peace of mind, he wanted to discuss the move with the archbishop of Toledo, Alfonso de Fonseca (1475–1534). The prelate received him kindly, approved his project, provided him substantial alms and a recommendation for his friends, and obtained a place in a college which he had personally founded at Salamanca.

THE PEDANTIC THEOLOGIANS AT SALAMANCA

Salamanca, the Athens of Spain! Although its university was less receptive to new ideas than Alcalá, it was a center for theological renewal. A generation of famous Dominicans taught there: Francisco de Vitoria (c. 1485–1546), the father of international law and a solid adversary of Erasmus; Melchor Cano, the author of the renowned *De locis theologicis* and the future unremitting censor of the *Spiritual Exercises* and of the Society; Tomás de Pedroche, haughty and pretentious. Íñigo, who counted on continuing his studies there, hardly profited from any of this. His lasted only two months, 25 days of which were spent in prison.

He arrived in the middle of July, and rejoined his four companions who had rented a small house. Right away, Íñigo set out to look for a confessor. He found one among the Dominicans of San Esteban. He would later regret this choice. After had had been in Salamanca ten or twelve days, the good confessor invited him to dine with the community: his colleagues wanted to get to know him and to hear his views on numerous topics. The following Sunday, after the meal, Íñigo, accompanied by Calisto, was invited to speak with the community. After the subprior had expressed his astonishment at Calisto's attire, he questioned Íñigo:

> 'Well, then, what is it you preach?' We do not preach,' replied the pilgrim, 'but we speak familiarly of spiritual things with a few, as one does after dinner, with those who invite us.' 'But,' asked the friar, 'what are the things you speak about; that is what we would like to know.' 'We speak,' answered the pilgrim. 'sometimes of one virtue, sometimes of another, to praise it; sometimes of one vice, sometimes of another, to condemn it.' You are not

educated,' observed the friar, 'and you speak of virtues and vices? No one can speak of these things except in two ways, either because he has studied, or through the Holy Spirit. You have not studied; therefore you speak through the Holy Spirit.'[10]

Seeing the trap, Íñigo refused to continue. The Dominican, now irritated, concluded "Well, remain here; we can easily see to it that you tell us all."[11] The community left the room, the doors were closed and the judges alerted. For three days, Íñigo and Calisto found themselves prisoners of the convent before being transported to the city jail, so closely chained to one another that one could not take a step without dragging along his companion in misfortune. When this became known in the city, people brought them something to sleep on and what was necessary for their sustenance. And the visits provided Íñigo with wonderful occasions to speak of God and to propose the spiritual exercises.

Íñigo was interrogated about the *Exercises*, theology and canon law by Francisco Frías (d. 1568), the bishop's vicar. Íñigo gave him all his papers, specifically the *Exercises*.[12] He was asked to explain the Trinity, the Blessed Sacrament, the first commandment, as he habitually did. Íñigo began by saying that he had studied little, but then became so talkative that they did not ask him anymore. One point in the *Exercises* caused serious difficulties: since he had not studied, how could he distinguish between mortal sin and venial sin?

Prison did not seem to bother him very much. To the men and women who asked him how he could tolerate imprisonment, he generally replied that "there are not bars enough or chains enough in Salamanca but I would desire more for God's love."[13] He even refused a possibility of escaping, and this led to a change in his prison regime. The verdict came after 22 days. No error was found in the *Exercises*. He could, thus, continue to teach catechism, but must refrain from defining what is a mortal or venial sin for four years, the time needed to finish his studies. When the judges manifested their goodwill and their satisfaction with a verdict favorable to him, Íñigo replied that he would observe the injunction as long as he was under the jurisdiction of Salamanca, but that he would not accept a sentence that obliged him to keep his mouth shut and thus prevented him from helping his neighbor as he considered it his duty to do since he had not been condemned.

Released from prison, Íñigo again pondered how he was going to continue. He remained certain of one thing and never once had second thoughts about it: he wanted to study in order to help others, and to gather together companions who shared his project. With this interdiction, another door had been slammed in his face. He decided to leave Salamanca to go to study in Paris. The warnings of his friends in Barcelona were not enough to make him renounce a project which seemed a bit crazy to others. At a time when the tension between the two kingdoms was at its height and war was ready to erupt, crossing France was a serious danger for a Spaniard. Was it not said that the French would roast them alive? Nothing happened. When Ignatius, in his old age, dictated his memoires, he added that "he saw no reason for being afraid."[14] So fifteen or twenty days after his release from prison, he set out alone for Paris, riding on a little donkey with only a few books as companions.

Why Paris? Certainly because its university was a reference point for all those who wanted to study the fine arts, philosophy and theology. But Íñigo had a more personal reason which Polanco mentioned.[15] Since he did not know French, he thought that Paris would provide fewer temptations for apostolic work. He was, in fact, beginning to realize that serious studies were incompatible with an all-consuming apostolic activity such as that which had occupied him until then. Later on, he would severely curb the apostolic impulses of students at the college of Coimbra and, in the *Constitutions of the Society*,[16] he reminded the reader that prayers and long meditations should not occupy much time and energy during the period of studies which should engage the whole person.

PARIS AND SERIOUS STUDIES

Íñigo arrived in Paris in the middle of winter, February 2, 1528. He found lodging in a house occupied by other Spaniards who helped him find his way around the large city. Since he thought that he had botched his prior studies and that he was seriously deficient in the basics, he decided to return to the study of humanities in a classroom with children, and to enroll in classes of Latin (grammar, rhetoric, metrics) at the Collège de Montaigu, on the left bank in the Latin Quarter. Thanks to assistance from his friends in Barcelona, he had enough money to assure his sustenance for a good two years. Unfortunately, he entrusted his finances to a Spaniard in his lodging who spent it all in a very short time. Unable to repay the sum, the swindler left for Spain. But he fell ill near Rouen and sent for Íñigo to help him out. After a serious inner struggle, Íñigo overcame his repugnance, and walked for three days barefoot without food or drink to bring aid to the Spaniard and help him embark. To judge by the importance he attributed to this episode in his memoirs, this gesture was particularly difficult.[17]

So Íñigo, as poor as ever, was again forced to beg, to abandon the house where he had been living, and to seek lodging at the hospice of Saint James, an accommodation for the pilgrims of Compostela situated on the other side of the Seine, three kilometers from the college. The timetables of the two establishments complicated his life. At Montaigu classes began before the doors of the hospice opened for the day and ended in the evening after they had been closed. Since he was obliged to miss hours of classes with the foreseeable results, he made little progress. He would have liked to have attached himself to the service of a professor as did other students while he continued his studies. Yet in spite of all his efforts he was unable to obtain such a position. A Spanish religious spoke to him of the generosity of rich Spanish businessmen in Flanders and counseled him to try his luck: it would be better to spend two months begging than to waste his time in Paris. So every year, during Lent and in summer, Íñigo traveled to Bruges and Antwerp; once he even crossed to England. He brought back not only enough to cover his expenses for the year, but also the friendship and respect of his sponsors who sent him bills of exchange so as to save him the trips.

Less burdened by financial worries, Íñigo took advantage of his situation to resume his apostolic activities: "he began to give himself more intensely than

usual to spiritual conversation."[18] When it was a question of winning souls
for Christ, his charity became creative: he helped poor students by soliciting
assistance for them from those who were better off. To encourage a doctor
to make the *Exercises,* he played against him and won.[19] To help a depressed
person come out of his sullenness, he did not have any qualms about dancing
and singing Basque songs.[20] His example and his activity led many students
to return to the sacraments or enter holy orders; others changed their life style
and chose poverty.[21]

Íñigo certainly exercised a real fascination over acquaintances whether they
were students, doctors, or teachers. Pedro Peralta, Juan de Castro and Amador
de Elduayen, three students to whom he had given the *Exercises,* had subsequently distributed their possessions, even their books, to the poor, and began
to beg and to live at the hospice. The story caused a commotion and the Spanish
colony was indignant. An armed expedition was organized to bring them back
to the University. Once they had finished their studies, they could do whatever
they wanted. Remarks and gossip about Íñigo circulated. He was making people
crazy![22] All this agitation aroused the attention of the Inquisition and the rector
of the Sainte-Barbe Collège, Master Diogo de Gouveia (c. 1471–1557), promised
to give him a good trashing on the next occasion. When he heard this, Íñigo
asked the Inquisitor to judge his case as soon as possible because he wanted to
start the liberal arts classes at the Sainte-Barbe Collège on October 1, the feast
of Saint Remigius (Rémy), and he did not want to waste time with such things.
In fact, he was not summoned and he began his studies as foreseen under the
direction of Master Juan de la Peña.

Another danger awaited him: every time he started to study, spiritual
thoughts distracted him. As in Barcelona, he could not escape their allure
and concentrate on his studies until he had promised a teacher that he would
not miss another class. Exteriorly, everything was tranquil; nobody gave him
any problems. But this exceptional change drew comments. When a professor
observed this, Íñigo retorted: "It is because I do not speak to anyone of the
things of God, but once the course is finished the old life will return."[23]

Three years later, in 1532, he received a bachelor of arts degree. He became
a graduate teacher in 1533; obtained his master's degree in 1534, and began
studying theology with the Dominicans of the convent of Saint Jacques. It was
around this time that he adopted the Latin form of his first name. Henceforth
he would no longer call himself Íñigo, but Ignatius. Traditionally the Society
of Jesus explained that Íñigo changed his name out of devotion to the martyr
Ignatius of Antioch. However, Ignatius is not the Latin equivalent of Íñigo
and there is no concrete evidence that he did so in homage to the martyr.[24]

What assessment can be made of these studies at Paris? Before he came to
Paris, Ignatius, on several occasions, alluded to his lack of formation. He had
not learned much at Alcalá and Salamanca because his apostolic undertakings,
and consequent legal issues left him little time for studies. In Paris, he val-
iantly went to work to make up for the time he had lost. Thus his formation
was essentially Parisian: humanities at Sainte-Barbe, liberal arts at Montaigu
College, theology with the Dominicans of Saint-Jacques. Difficulties were not
lacking, however, even if, according to Laínez, he applied himself more than
his fellow students and progressed normally.[25] Nadal indicated three major
handicaps which perturbed his studies: great poverty, precarious health, and
distractions due to the intensity of his spiritual life.[26]

Although he was not particularly attracted to studying, Ignatius, not
without difficulty and thanks to the help of his friends, acquired a formation
sufficient for the realization of his project of serving God by helping others.
He was more intuitive than speculative; he did not have an impressive eru-
dition, but possessed iron willpower, an extraordinary memory, and a vivid
imagination which was easily aroused. At the end of his biographical sketch,
Laínez added that Ignatius stood out because of his profound knowledge of
spiritual things—even the most abstract; because he was a man of counsel;
because he showed a great prudence in the way he did things; and because
he had the gift of discernment.[27] Other witnesses evoke the wisdom and
rapidity of his replies.

Notes

1. *Saint Ignatius's Own Story, p. 51, num. 7.*

2. *Fontes narrativi*, vol. 1, pp. 170–71. See also Barton T. Geger, S.J., "The *First* First Companions," *Studies in the Spirituality of* Jesuits, 44/2 (2012): pp. 10–12

3. See Stefania Pastore, "Unwise Paths: Ignatius Loyola and the Years of Alcalá de Henares," in Maryks, *Companion*, pp. 25–43.

4. Diego entered the Society in 1540. Miguel was the official printer and publisher of the university.

5. Manuel Miona, at the time a professor at Alcalá, entered the Society in 1545.

6. *Remembering Íñigo*, pp. 58–59, nums. 97–98.

7. *Saint Ignatius's Own Story*, p. 43, num. 60.

8. *Fontes documenti*, pp. 319–49. Cfo a partial translation of the process in Ignace de Loyola, *Texte autographe des Exercises spirituels et documents contemporains (1526–1615)* (Paris: Desclee de Brouwer, 1986), pp. 199–207.

9. *Saint Ignatius's Own Story*, p. 42, num. 59.

10. *Saint Ignatius's Own Story*, p. 47, num. 65.

11. *Saint Ignatius's Own Story*, p. 48, num. 66.

12. This was the first time that Ignatius mentions the *Exercises* in the form of a written text.

13. *Saint Ignatius's Own Story*, p. 50, num. 69.

14. *Saint Ignatius's Own Story*, p. 51, num. 72.

15. *Fontes narrativi*, vol. 1, p. 117.

16. *Constitutions*, p. 183, num. 340.

17. *Saint Ignatius's Own Story*, pp. 54–55, num. 79.

18. *Saint Ignatius's Own Story*, p. 53, num. 77.

19. *Fontes narrativi*, vol. 4, p. 875.

20. Considering that this episode was not in line with his edifying image of Ignatius, Ribadeneira does not mention the comical scene. See García-Villoslada, *San Ignacio de Loyola*, p. 343.

21. *Life of Ignatius*, pp. 21–22.

22. See Geger, "*First* First Companions," pp. 12–14.

23. *Saint Ignatius's Own Story*, p. 57, num. 82.

24. See Hugo Rahner, S.J., *La genèse des Exercises* (Paris: Desclée de Brouwer, 1989), p.76.

25. *Fontes narrativi*, vol. 1, p. 100.

26. *Fontes narrativi*, vol. 2, p. 198.

27. *Fontes narrativi*, vol. 1, p. 136.

X

FRIENDS UNITED BY A SAME IDEAL

According to Polanco, Íñigo first found companions in Barcelona, men interested in joining him in his project of "reforming the faults he saw in the divine service," of living according to the example of the apostles, and of being "trumpets of Jesus Christ."[1] Under his guidance, Calisto, Cáceres, Arteaga, and Juanico taught catechism and gave the exercises. Others recognized the existence of this distinct group and even referred to it as their "company" (Society). At Acalá and Salamanca, his companions shared his lot. Like him, they were pursued by the Inquisition, condemned to change their vestments, and forbidden to preach until they finished their studies. When he left for Paris, Íñigo asked them to remain at Salamanca while he explored the possibilities of their following him to Paris to continue their studies.[2] The project proved more difficult than he had expected. In spite of his efforts to find subsidies for their studies, his companions did not join him. Juanico became a monk, and the three others abandoned their life-style to follow careers, not always edifying, in the service of the Church.[3] The embryo of the Society was aborted, but it would soon be reborn under more viable conditions.

His entry into the Collège of Sainte-Barbe in 1529 to study liberal arts under the direction of Juan de la Peña was providential. His master found lodgings for him in a chamber with two other students, fifteen years younger and already well-advanced in their studies: the first, a Savoyard, Pierre Favre (1506–1546), born in Villaret, a hamlet in the commune of Grand-Bornand, at that time in the diocese of Geneva, and Francisco Javier (Francis Xavier) (1506–1552), from Navarre, born in the chateau of Javier. Ignatius and Favre got

along well from the start. Ignatius helped him out materially, and Favre repaid
him by helping him with his studies. Soon a deep friendship united the old
student and his young tutor. Favre was impressed by the spiritual insights of
Ignatius and confided his doubts to him. He was tormented by scruples and
temptations against chastity and was questioning himself about his future. The
counsels of Ignatius enabled him to find that peace again. In his "Memoirs,"
the tender and gentle Savoyard reminisced:

> On January 10, 1529, at the age of twenty-three, I became a bachelor of
> arts and after Easter was awarded the licentiate under Master Juan de la
> Peña, now a doctor of Medicine . . . . That year Íñigo entered the same
> Collège Sainte-Barbe and lodged in the same room as ourselves, intending
> to begin the course in arts on the coming feast of St. Remy [Remigius]; our
> master (mentioned above) was to give the course. Eternally blessed be all
> this that divine providence arranged for my good and for my salvation. For
> after providence decreed that I was to be the instructor of that holy man,
> we conversed at first about secular matters, then about spiritual things.
> There followed a life in common in which we two shared the same room,
> the same table, and the same purse. As time passed, he became my master
> in spiritual things and gave me a method of raising myself to a knowledge
> of the divine will and of myself. In the end we became one in desire and
> will and one in a firm resolve to take up that life we lead today—we, the
> present or future members of this Society of which I am unworthy.[4]

Pierre Favre made the *Exercises* under the direction of Ignatius. Later, Ignatius would say that of all those he knew in the Society, Favre was the best for
giving the *Exercises*.[5] Ordained in 1534, he would become the first priest of the
Society of Jesus.

    With Francis Xavier, the contact was more difficult. The young and bril-
liant noble, rather worldly, good at sports, was an idealist who only dreamed
of claiming his rights of nobility and having a career. His origins had opened

the gates of Paris for him and he was admired by the students. The arrival of this already older student in their room, who was too pious and critical and, moreover, allied to the Oñaz clan, was more of a bother to him than anything else. So he did not miss an occasion to mock or make fun of him in spite of the many kindnesses which Ignatius showed to him. Finally, touched by the friendship of Favre for Ignatius, Xavier gave in. Later on, he made the *Exercises*, and decided to join in the project of Ignatius. Polanco is supposed to have said: "One day I heard this great molder of men, Ignatius, say that the toughest dough that he ever had to kneed at the beginnings was this young Francis Xavier."[6] In his life of Ignatius, Ribadeneira says nothing of the difficulties with Xavier!

Other companions from the student body will soon follow.[7] First, two friends, Diego Laínez (20 years old), an extremely gifted young man, already with a doctorate of Liberal Arts, and Alfonso Salmerón (1515–1585)[8] who came from Alcalá where his and Íñigo's paths had crossed. Then Nicolás Alonso (1511–1590), known as Bobadilla from the name of the village where he was born, He was a young man of peasant stock, solid but joyous and extroverted who had heard that Ignatius was helping students in difficulty. Following Ignatius's advice, he went on to theological studies and, thanks to his help, Bobadilla obtained the post of regent in the Collège of Calvi. Finally, a pious Portuguese, possessed of a lively disposition but subject to bouts of melancholy, Simão Rodrigues de Acebedo (1510–1579), who studied at Sainte-Barbe. After making the *Exercises* under the direction of Ignatius, these students came to share a same ideal: they wanted to follow Christ and labor to "help souls." Ignatius did not indoctrinate them. Being careful not to impose himself between them and the Lord, he simply helped them to find the will of God in themselves, as he recommended to anyone directing the *Exercises*—a counsel which aroused the anger of Melchor Cano:

> The director of the Exercises ought not to urge the exercitant more to poverty or any promise than to the contrary, nor to one state of life or way of

living more than to another. . . . But while one is engaged in the Spiritual
Exercises, it is more suitable and much better that the Creator and Lord
in person communicate Himself to the devout soul in quest of the divine
will, that He inflame it with His love of Himself, and dispose it for the way
in which it could better serve God in the future.[9]

On August 15, 1534, in Our Lady of the Martyrs Church in Montmartre,
in the course of a Mass celebrated by Pierre Favre, the only priest of the group,
after having gone to confession and having taken communion, they all pronounced vows of poverty and chastity, which they intended to renew annually
on the same date. They had absolutely no intention of entering a religious
order, and even less of founding one. Laínez wrote: "Our intention at Paris
was not to found a congregation, but to consecrate ourselves in poverty to
the service of God Our Lord and to the service of our neighbors by preaching,
serving in hospitals etc."[10] For the moment, they only had one project in mind:
a pilgrimage to Jerusalem where, if possible, they would consecrate themselves
to the evangelization of the Muslims and die for their faith in Christ. Some
(Ignatius, Laínez and Xavier) planned to remain in Jerusalem definitively,
while others (Favre and Rodrigues) envisaged returning. Finally, they agreed
to decide by a majority of votes once they were there.

Having learned from Ignatius's previous failure, the friends made previ-
sions that, in the case they would not be able to remain in Jerusalem, or if a
war prevented them from going to Palestine, they would wait a year before
considering themselves freed from their vow. In such a case, they would go to
Rome and place themselves at the disposition of the Vicar of Christ so that he
might "make use of them wherever he thought it would be more to God's glory
and the good of souls."[11] Ignatius did not know, any more than his companions
did, where all this was going to lead them. Contrary to common belief, this
was not a strategy designed to implement a preestablished plan. The Society
of Jesus was not born on Montmartre. Jerónimo Nadal noted: "At that time,
when he [Ignatius] was in Paris, he followed the guidance of the Spirit and

did not try to get ahead of it. In this way, he was gently led towards a goal that he ignored and which he never dreamed of when the Society was founded; he advanced towards it, little by little, without knowing where he was going, in the simplicity of his heart anchored in Christ."[12]

As the group became more and more united and in so doing attracted attention, they were called the "Íñiguistas." The men shared an ideal; they were frequently seen together; they gathered regularly in the house of one or another for discussions and meals. On Sundays they went to the countryside near the Carthusian monastery of Vauvert where they passed the day in discussions and religious offices: five Spaniards, a Savoyard and a Portuguese, all masters of liberal arts and fairly proficient in theology. In a letter to Jean de Verdolay from Venice dated July 24, 1537, Ignatius, speaking of his companions, wrote that they were "friends in the Lord."[13] Even though Ignatius only used this term once and it does not appear in any foundational text of the Society, the expression conveyed quite well the nature of the bond which united the Parisian students. Above and beyond their diverse origins and their different opinions, it was indeed friendship which united them in "a one and the same thought and will, which was to seek out the good pleasure and perfect will of God according to the designs of their vocation."[14]

Notes

1. *Fontes narrativi*, vol. 1, p. 170.

2. See Philippe Lécrivain, S.J, *Paris in the Time of Ignatius of Loyola (1528–1535)* (St. Louis: The Institute of Jesuit Sources, 2011).

3. See Geger, "*First* First Companions," pp. 11–12.

4. *The Spiritual Writings of Pierre Favre*, ed. and trans. by Edmond C. Murphy, S.J., Martin E. Palmer, S.J., and John W. Padberg, S.J. (St. Louis: The Institute of Jesuit Sources, 1996), pp. 64–65, nums. 7–8.

5. *Remembering Íñigo*, p. 130, num. 226. See also Paul Beghen, S.J., "Peter Favre as Director of the Spiritual Exercises: The Case of Peter Canisius," in McCoog, *Ite inflammate omnia*, pp. 71–84.

6. *Fontes narrativi*, vol. 3, p. 282. The French Jesuit Émond Auger

mentioned Polanco's statement in his recollections of Ignatius.

7. See José García de Castro Valdés, "Ignatius of Loyola and His First Companions," in Maryks, *Companion*, pp. 66–83.

8. See William V. Bangert, S.J., *Claude Jay and Alfonso Salmerón: Two Early Jesuits* (Chicago: Loyola Press, 1985).

9. *Spiritual Exercises*, p. 6, num. 15.

10. *Fontes narrativi*, vol. 1, p. 110. See also Polanco's comment on p. 185.

11. *Saint Ignatius's Own Story*, p. 59, num. 85.

12. *Fontes narrativi*, vol. 2, p. 252.

13. *Letters and Instructions,* pp. 28–31.

14. "The Deliberation of Our First Fathers," John Codur, S.J., and Peter Faber, S.J., trans. Dominic Maruca, S.J., *Woodstock Letters* 95 (1966), p. 328, num. 1. See also Javier Osuna, S.J., *Friends in the Lord* (London: Way Publications, 1974).

XI

The Therapy of Native Air

Ignatius's health had always been precarious. During his stay in Paris, after a period of respite, his stomach pains returned worse than ever with severe crises and fevers every two weeks. None of the doctors consulted and none of the remedies tried calmed him. The faculty recommended that he seek health by breathing his native air. The counsels of the doctors and the insistence of his companions finally persuaded him to try this therapy. He also used the occasion to settle some pending affairs concerning his Spanish companions. He would then set out for Venice where he would rejoin his companions after they had completed their studies in 1537 for their journey to the Holy Land.[1] Meanwhile Pierre Favre played the role of big brother.

At the moment of departure, Ignatius learned that the Inquisition was still interested in him. Someone in Paris had denounced him. For his peace of mind, he asked the inquisitor, the Dominican Valentin Liévin, to pass judgement without delay because Ignatius was on the point of leaving for Spain. The inquisitor asked to see "what he had written in the Exercises." After going over them with a fine-tooth comb, he praised them, and even asked for a copy for his personal use. Ignatius gave him one. But this kindness was not enough for Ignatius; he wanted a formal judgement. This was carried out before witnesses and registered by a court clerk. He could then leave Paris in peace, after having studied there for seven years and two months. Once again he went off "alone" on a little horse that his companions procured for him.[2]

His stay in his native province aroused tensions within his family. Ignatius chose to lodge at the hospice with the poor and to beg for his needs. He wanted to speak of the things of God, teach catechism to children, and preach on Sundays and feast days. His brother Martín, now lord of Loyola, who was ashamed of his life style as unworthy of a Loyola, and convinced that nobody would come to his catechism lessons, tried by all possible means to convince him to accept the hospitality of the family home. In vain! Ignatius was adamant: he would continue to live at the hospice with the poor and even if he had only one student that would be enough for him. In fact, people began to gather in crowds to listen to him; some even came from far off. Since the church became too small to accommodate all these people, the preaching continued outside. Witnesses relate that some of the audience climbed up on trees and walls and that the surrounding meadows were being trampled.[3] In public, Ignatius spoke with a high-pitched and loud voice, which carried a great distance; he used a simple language, without oratorical flourishes. His word made an impression; the expression of an interior fire, it is convincing and demands respect.[4]

The fruit of these sermons was notable. People abandoned their life of sin and went to confession; enemies were reconciled; card games were forbidden and, from now on, justice pursued women who had publically acknowledged themselves to be concubines of priests. As always, Ignatius was concerned about the lot of the poor: "he saw to it that some provision was officially and regularly made for the poor." Finally, at his request, the bells would ring three times a day for the *Angelus,* as was the custom in Rome, "so that the people should pray."[5]

At the beginning of his stay in his homeland, his health improved, but sickness soon caught up with him again. He had hardly recovered when he set out to visit the families of his companions, and to put their affairs in order. As was his custom, he set out without any money and on foot. Another disgrace for the family! His brother, furious, obliged him to take a horse. Ignatius accepted the offer, but only to the limits of the province!

He visited the family of Laínez in Almazán, in Navarre; he met the brother of Xavier; at Sigüenza he greeted the parents of Salmerón; at Valencia, after having been reunited with a retreatant from Paris, he embarked for Genoa.

The crossing was very shaky to the point of leading him to the doors of death. Between Genoa and Bologna, he thought that his last hour had come. Lost in a ravine, directly above a river, he was only able to advance by crawling, with the risk of falling into the void at any moment. Years later, when evoking his memories, Ignatius confessed that this was the greatest fatigue and the greatest physical suffering he had ever endured. After a short stay at Bologna, just enough time to fall ill, he left for Venice "using always the same method of travel."[6]

NOTES

1. The companions were scheduled to depart for Venice on January 25, 1537. Because of the threat of war, their departure was moved up to November 15, 1536.

2. *Saint Ignatius's Own Story*, pp. 59–61, nums. 86–87.

3. *Scripta de Sancto Ignatio de Loyola* (2 vols., Madrid: Lopez del Horno, 1904–1918), vol. 2, pp. 191, 217.

4. See García-Villoslada, *San Ignacio de Loyola*, p. 375.

5. *Saint Ignatius's Own Story*, pp. 61–62, nums. 88–89.

6. *Saint Ignatius's Own Story*, p. 63, nums. 90–91.

XII

Venice and the Priesthood

At Venice, Ignatius dedicated himself to spiritual conversations and giving the *Exercises* to persons of quality. He even won over a new Spanish companion: the bachelor of arts Diego Hoces (c. 1490–1538) of Málaga, who showed up with a library of theological manuals in case this strange spiritual advisor would teach him some suspected doctrine.[1] After all, was there not a rumor that Ignatius had been burned in effigy in Spain and at Paris? Rumors followed him to the city of the Doges. There a new investigation was opened and once again the judges exonerated him.

Meanwhile, at Paris, three other students joined the companions after having made the *Exercises* under the guidance of Pierre Favre: a second Savoyard, Claude Jay (1504–1552) from Mieussy;[2] a Picard, Pascase Broët (1500–1562) from Betracourt; and a Provençal, Jean Codure (1508–1541) from Sayne. The group of nine companions arrived at Venice two years later in the middle of winter, after an epic journey through Lorraine, Southern Germany and Switzerland, regions infested with soldiers and heretics. The inns represented real dangers for faith and morals, and chance encounters with married priests and reformed ministers were a rude test.

Several months later, his companions set out for Rome to seek the pope's blessing for their voyage to Jerusalem. Ignatius prudently did not accompany them; instead he awaited their return at Venice. Ignatius avoided the trip because he did not want to risk an encounter with Dr. Pedro Ortiz, Emperor Charles V's ambassador to the pope. Ortiz had earlier denounced Ignatius's activities among the students of Paris.[3] Ignatius also wanted to avoid the formidable Gian Pietro, Cardinal Carafa (1476–1559), cofounder of the Theatines, with whom he had previously clashed.[4]

Divided into three groups of mixed nationalities, the companions traveled by foot and begged for their sustenance as Ignatius always did. When they returned, they brought back not only the pontifical documents authorizing their voyage to Jerusalem with the possibility of remaining there if they so desired, but also the authorization to be ordained priests by any bishop whatsoever. The pope also gave them letters of credit worth 200 to 300 crowns for their journey.[5]

On June 24, 1537, Ignatius and his friends—with the exception of Favre who was already a priest and Salmerón who was still too young—were ordained priests by Vincenzo Nigusanti, bishop of Arbe, today known as Rab, an island off the Dalmatian coast "under the title of poverty."[6] All planned to celebrate their first Mass in Palestine. At the end of September, however, because their voyage was delayed by the war between Venice and the Turks, the companions celebrated their first Mass in Venice—with the exception of Ignatius who "had made up his mind after taking orders to wait a year before saying Mass, preparing himself and praying our Lady to place him with her Son."[7] Meanwhile, he received communion from Favre or Laínez.[8] This additional delay of 18 months raised questions even among the first generation of Jesuits. When Laínez asked Ribadeneira if he knew something about it, the latter evasively replied that "Father must have had some secret reason for doing this."[9] Perhaps a reason can be found in the Christology of Ignatius. In the past, guided by his reading of the *Vita Christi* by Ludolph of Saxony, he undertook the journey to Palestine in the hope of physically putting his footsteps in those of Jesus. Since the sacrament put him in contact with the humanity of Christ who carried his cross and called him to follow him, he wanted to celebrate his first Mass in the very land of Jesus where he had shed his blood. Thus after three months of waiting, as his companions, convinced of the impossibility of traveling to Palestine, decided to celebrate their first Mass, Ignatius had not abandoned hope that he could make journey. Fifteen months later, after the war had definitively cancelled the trip and Ignatius was certain that the Lord wanted him in Rome, he celebrated Mass for the first time at the Basilica of Santa Maria Maggiore where there was a relic of the manger. Since entry into the Holy Land was closed to him, he still found, at Rome, a place where there was a material relic of the presence of God's humanity.[10]

As they waited, the companions divided themselves into groups of two or three to make a retreat in the region. Ignatius went apart with Favre and Laínez to San Pietro in Vivarolo, an old monastery in ruins, without doors or windows. There they slept on straw mats, begged for bread which, more than once, they did not receive, and spent the day in prayer. After Jean Codure joined them, they decided to preach in public places. Their success was such that, from then on, they lacked nothing. As had been the case at Manresa previously, Ignatius, very consoled, received many mystical graces at San Pedro, above all when he thought of his priesthood, and prepared to celebrate his first Mass. Always attentive to others, even though he himself was suffering from a fever, he hastened to the bedside of Simão Rodrigues who was sick at Bassano 30 miles away. Favre, who accompanied him, could hardly keep up the pace.

At the end of this quasi-retreat of forty days, they met again in Venice. They decided that they would disperse throughout the university cities of northern Italy as they still awaited their departure for Palestine. One practical question still had to be resolved: the identity of their group. How were they to reply to those who asked them who they were? Well, since they had no other leader than Jesus Christ whom they had decided to follow, they would reply that they were "the Society of Jesus."[11] They were not "Íñiguistas" because they were not following Íñigo but rather Christ. This name led to some confusion. The first Jesuits defined their group in that they followed Christ as his companions similar to the apostles, but popular opinion, misled by the fact that Ignatius had previously been a soldier, understood this appellation in military terms. Ribadeneira himself promoted the misunderstanding in the measure because of his frequent insistence on this "sacred militia" formed by "the soldiers of this holy and blessed captain" engaged in a struggle against the Reformation.[12] The name that had been chosen will soon find a supreme confirmation on the road to Rome, in a little sanctuary of La Storta. Melchor Cano, the irreconcilable adversary, was indignant that anyone could have the hubris of putting himself on the same level as Christ. This betrayed a certain smugness on the part of these Jesuits.

NOTES

1. On Hoces and other temporary companions, see Geger, "*First* First Companions," pp. 14–21.

2. See Bangert, *Claude Jay and Alfonso Salmerón*.

3. Ignatius would conduct Dr. Ortiz through the *Exercises* in 1538. Ortiz became a great admirer and supporter.

4. The Theatines were the first congregation of regular clerics, founded in 1524 by Gaetano Tiene (1480–1547, canonized in 1671), and Carafa, the future pope Paul IV.

5. *Saint Ignatius's Own Story*, pp. 64–65, nums. 92–93.

6. *Saint Ignatius's Own Story*, p. 65, num. 93.

7. *Saint Ignatius's Own Story*, pp. 66–67, num. 96.

8. *Fontes narrativi*, vol. 1, p. 133.

9. Leturia, *Estudios ignacianos*, vol. 1, p. 224.

10. See Pierre Emonet, S.J., "Ignace et l'eucharistie," *Christus* 171 (July, 1996), pp. 348–57.

11. *Fontes narrativi*, vol. 1, p. 203. In a less sober narrative with pretensions at edification, Ribadeneira explained that the name of the Society of Jesus was chosen by Ignatius after a mystical experience in the chapel of La Storta (*Life of Ignatius*, pp. 97–99).

12. *Life of Ignatius*, pp. 4–5, 8–10, 99.

XIII

ROME RATHER THAN JERUSALEM

While the other companions were ministering in the university cities of Northern Italy—Bologna, Ferrara, Padua—Ignatius, Favre and Laínez set out for Rome to put themselves at the disposition of the pope as they had planned. On the way, Ignatius experienced a great consolation. When they were within sight of Rome, fourteen kilometers from the city, on the via Cassia, at the place called La Storta, as he was praying in a chapel and asking the Madonna "to place him with her Son,"[1] he clearly saw the Father Himself putting him with His Son. The change that he experienced was such that it left no doubt that this grace came from God. Ignatius himself says nothing more about this. Laínez, who was accompanying him, is more talkative in an exhortation addressed to the Jesuits of Rome:

> When we were going to Rome, along the road to Siena, our Father had numerous spiritual experiences, especially in the most holy Eucharist which he received each day and which was given to him by Master Pierre Favre or myself who celebrated Mass every day while he did not. He told me that it seemed to him that God the Father was imprinting in his heart these words: "I will be propitious to you in Rome." And not knowing what that meant, our Father said: "I don't know what is going to happen to us; maybe we will be crucified in Rome." Then, on another occasion, he said to me that he seemed to see Christ carrying the cross and the Father alongside him who was saying: "I want you to take this one for your servant." And then Jesus took him and said: "I want you to serve us."[2]

The vision of Christ carrying his cross and inviting Ignatius to follow him forewarned him of difficulties awaiting them in Rome. When he arrived at the city, Ignatius confided to his companions that he had seen the windows closed, a fact which he interpreted as an announcement of the contradictions which they would soon confront, among others the gossip about their relationships with women.[3] They would need to show a great deal of prudence.

More Legal Proceedings

Life in the Eternal City was far from restful. The companions preached, heard confessions, taught catechism to the children at different churches in Rome, gave the *Exercises*, and provided assistance to the poor. The men who did not know Italian struggled to make themselves understood. Ignatius, who was not very good at languages, communicated in a mixture of Latin, Italian and Spanish. The result made young Pedro de Ribadeneira, who was charged with correcting his grammatical faults, cringe and give up: they were simply too numerous.[4] Laínez and Salmerón taught Holy Scripture and theology at the university.

Problems quickly arose and, as usual, they ended up in court. Miguel Landívar, an ex-candidate and a bit of a psychopath, who had been accepted but eventually excluded from the group, calumniated Ignatius who finally brought the case to the governor.[5] This led to the expulsion of the guilty party from Rome. A more serious quarrel involved Favre and Laínez and an Augustinian monk Agostino Mainardi, a brilliant orator and crypto-Lutheran whose sermons touched on certain themes that the companions belived to be heretical. Two Spaniard supporters of the preacher, Francisco Mudarra and someone named Barrera, countered by circulating the rumor that Ignatius and his companions had been pursued by the Inquisition in Spain, Paris, and Venice because of their doctrine, and that they in fact endorsed Protestant teachings and propagated heresy through the *Spiritual Exercises*. The calumniators retracted and the case was closed. But Ignatius was not at all satisfied with this dismissal and instead demanded a formal judgement which the legate and others deemed unnecessary. Obstinate, he personally appealed to the pope and asked that justice be done.[6] Not one to bear grudges, Ignatius made great efforts to free Mudarra, "the greatest opponent of the Society at the beginning," when he fell into the hands of the Inquisition.[7]

In a letter to Pietro Contarini, dated December 2, 1538, Ignatius explained his determination to obtain a judgement.[8] He insisted on pursuing the matter against the advice of the judges, his friends, and even his companions, in order to prove the orthodoxy of their doctrine and the integrity of their life. He was willing to brush aside insults, humiliations, criticisms, and mockeries, but when the rectitude of their teaching was questioned and their lifestyle judged unacceptable, he would not compromise. At each occasion, he demanded a formal sentence and was not satisfied with a simple dismissal. A demonstration of orthodoxy is not an end in itself, but an essential ingredient in their project "to help souls." Ignatius had dedicated his life to accompanying persons on their journey, to assisting them with the discovery of the will of God. In such troubled times, with so many heresies or suspected opinions running wild, he did not want to risk misleading his neighbor. This rectitude, maintained in spite of everything, reflected his fidelity to Christ and his respect for the people whom he sought to serve.

Care for the Poor

Besides their ministry of the Word, the companions cared for the poor and the sick. They visited them, tended to their needs, established charitable institutions, and collaborated with existing institutions. Difficulties and challenges did not impede Ignatius. In 1543, after he had become superior general of the Society, he set up catechumenates for converted Jews. Despite widespread public opposition to "New Christians" in Spain and elsewhere, Ignatius supplicated the pope on their behalf so that they would not lose their hereditary rights and the possession of their properties.[9] That same year, in spite of the skepticism of his friends, he established the House of Saint Martha (*Casa Santa Marta*) for repentant prostitutes. Within four years nearly, 300 women found refuge there. Their now frustrated clients spread diverse rumors about Ignatius. Once again Ignatius had recourse to the judges to defend his and his companions' reputations. To save the daughters of prostitutes from misery and to enable them to marry honorably, he established the Confraternity of Destitute Virgins (*Conservatorio delle Virgini Miserabili*).[10] He also collaborated with the establishment of homes for orphans. The activity of the companions during the famine of the winter of 1538–1539 was even more spectacular. According to Polanco, Jesuits provided sanctuary for as many as 400 poor persons to whom they offered a roof, fire, food, a bed or a straw mattress to sleep. At the same time they catechized their guests. Wealthy persons assisted the companions by providing clothes and food. A social service was organized to provide for some 3000 persons while the famine lasted. An attempt to set up a more structured and durable organization failed due to regrettable opposition.[11]

In his concern that no sick person die without religious succor, Ignatius had revived—admittedly under a more moderate form—an ancient decree of Pope Innocent III (c. 1160–1216, r. 1198–1216) which denied medical assistance to any sick person who refused the sacraments of the dying. Such a measure would be judged unacceptable today, but Ignatius's astonishing initiative may find some justification in the contemporaneous social and religious context. Before he intervened with the ecclesiastical authorities, Ignatius had consulted a group of competent experts who approved of his venture with the argument that the common and universal good took precedence over individual and particular good.[12] Ignatius had always been sensitive towards this argument, but it is difficult to reconcile it with individual, personal rights as they would later be defined.

At the Disposition of the Pope

Far from being a calculated strategy, the decision to place themselves at the disposition of the pope was simply an alternative if their original project was frustrated. As the companions realized their crossing to the Holy Land would be definitively barred, they became aware that their Jerusalem, the place where Christ became incarnate, would henceforth be the whole world. Nadal, who had a knack for well-honed expressions which would later be called "sound bites," wrote: "The world is our home."[13] Since they could not travel to their preferred holy place, they turned towards another space to follow and serve Christ—the concrete world with its profane political and social structures in which people lived and worked But where to go in a universe becoming ever more vast? What needed to be reformed? What was most urgent? So as not to go astray, the companions decided to ask someone who, from an elevated position, had an overall view of apostolic needs: the pope. For this reason they placed themselves at his disposition: to be sent where their service would be most useful and necessary. Through their vow of obedience, the Jesuits did not pretend to organize themselves as an elite troop, like the mercenaries of the pope, even if, later on, after the Society's 1814 Restoration, they performed this role too easily. Contrary to what Ribadeneira insinuated, they did not want to oppose Luther and the heretics who refused obedience to Rome.[14] They simply wanted to be mobile missionaries, ready to be useful in the reform of the Church anywhere in the world, wherever the need was most urgent. The choice of mobility in a horizontal universe explained their badly misunderstood approach. Pierre Favre elaborated on this in a letter written in Ignatius's name on November 23, 1538, to Diogo de Gouveia who, in the name of the Portuguese king, had requested Jesuits for the Indies:

> All of us, in so far as we are members of this Society, have put ourselves at the disposition of the Sovereign Pontiff in that he is responsible for the universal harvest of Christ. In making our offering, we have informed him that we are ready to obey in everything that he thinks he should command us in the name of Christ. So if he sends us where you desire us to be, we will go with joy. We have made this promise to submit ourselves to his judgement and to his will for the good reason that we believe he best knows the needs of Christianity.[15]

The *Constitutions* specifies:

> *The intention of the fourth vow pertaining to the pope was not to designate a*
> *particular place but to have the members distributed throughout the various*
> *parts of the world. For those who first united to form the Society were from*
> *different provinces and realms and did not know into which regions they were*
> *to go, whether among the faithful or the unbelievers; and therefore, to avoid*
> *erring in the path of the Lord, they made that promise or vow in order that*
> *His Holiness might distribute them the greater glory to God. They did this in*
> *conformity with their intention to travel throughout the whole world . . . .*[16]

When Ignatius and his companions arrived at Rome in November, 1538, to place themselves at the disposition of the pope, the city was buzzing about the splendor surrounding the marriage of Ottavio Farnese (1524–1586), Duke of Parma and grandson of Pope Paul III (1468–1549, r. 1534–1549) to Margaret of Parma (1522–1586), illegitimate daughter of Charles V. They respected the pope and recognized him as the Supreme Shepherd, the guide who oversaw the whole world and the whole Church. Ignatius would not tolerate any criticism of him from any Jesuit.[17] There is nothing servile in his attitude, simply the conviction that "For I must be convinced that in Christ our Lord, the bridegroom, and in His spouse the Church, only one Spirit holds sway, which governs and rules for the salvation of souls."[18] But he remained free. He was convinced that it was possible to know the will of God without any mediation, even pontifical, and he would not hesitate to defend his own insights and proposals with a respectful tenacity before Pope Paul IV who believed that he was correcting Ignatius's understanding of religious life by imposing conventual practices on the Society.

Ignatius knew four popes. Confidence may have characterized his relations with Paul III and Julius III (1487–1555, r. 1550–1555). He was especially friendly with Marcellus II (1501–1555, r. April 1555). But relations with Paul IV, the Carafa pope, were extremely tense. Both had strong personalities, were deeply concerned about Church reform, and founded new religious orders. At the beginning, Gian Pietro Carafa hoped to merge his Theatines with Ignatius's companions, a project doomed by their different understanding of religious life. In a convoluted letter, not lacking in audacity and perhaps ingenuity, Ignatius criticized the life-style of the Theatines, and expressed doubts about their future.[19] A vexed Carafa never forgave him and let him know it. On the day of his papal election, Ignatius trembled all over.[20] Paul IV, who in addition detested the Spanish, even went so far as to order a search of the house of Ignatius, suspecting it of being an arsenal and a hideout of his opponents.

Notes

1. *Saint Ignatius's Own Story*, p. 67, num. 96.

2. *Fontes narrativi*, vol. 2, p. 133. See also Bangert, *Jerome Nadal*, pp. 250–52 for different accounts of this vision.

3. *Saint Ignatius's Own Story*, p. 67, num. 97.

4. *Life of Ignatius*, pp.157–58.

5. Geger, "*First* First Companions," pp. 16–19.

6. *Life of Ignatius*, pp. 105–109.

7. *Remembering Íñigo*, pp. 183–84, num. 314. See also Pastore, "Unwise Paths"; and Sabina Pavone, "A Saint under Trial: Ignatius of Loyola between Alcalá and Rome," in Maryks, *Companion*, pp. 45–64.

8. *Letters and Instructions*, pp. 34–35.

9. *Life of Ignatius*, pp. 171–72. On recently baptized Jews, see O'Malley, *First Jesuits*, pp. 188–92.

10. On Jesuit confraternities, see Lance Lazar, *Working in the Vineyard of the Lord: Jesuit Confraternities in Early Modern Italy* (Toronto: University of Toronto Press, 2005). On sodalities, see Elder Mullan, *The Sodality of Our Lady: Studied in the Documents* (New York: PJ Kennedy & Sons, 1912).

11. *Fontes narrativi*, vol. 1, pp. 199–200.

12. Loyola to Marcello, Cardinal Cervini, Rome, 24 June 1543, *Epistolae et instructiones*, vol. 1, pp. 261–67.

13. See John W. O'Malley, S.J., "To Travel to Any Part of the World: Jerónimo Nadal and the Jesuit Vocation," *Studies in the Spirituality of Jesuits* 16/2 (1984) (reprinted in *Saints or Devils Incarnate?*, pp. 147–64).

14. *Fontes narrativi*, vol. 4, p. 715.

15. *Letters and Instructions*, pp. 32–34.

16. *Constitutions*, p. 268, num. 605. See also John W. O'Malley, S.J., "The Fourth Vow in Its Ignatian Context," *Studies in the Spirituality of Jesuits* 15/1 (1983), and John W. Padberg, S.J., "Ignatius, the Popes, and Realistic Reverence," *Studies in the Spirituality of Jesuits* 25/3 (1993).

17. *Remembering Íñigo*, pp. 56–57, nums. 94–95.

18. *Spiritual Exercises*, p. 160, num. 365.

19. Loyola to Carafa, Venice 1536, *Sancti Ignatii de Loyola Societatis Iesu fundatoris epistolae et instructiones* (12 vols., reprinted, Rome: Institutum Historicum Societatis Iesu, 1964–1968), vol. 1, pp. 114–18.

20. *Remembering Íñigo*, pp. 55–56, num. 93.

XIV

An Order Too Innovative

By a vow, the companions had committed themselves to be at the pope's disposition, to be sent wherever he judged that they might be most useful. A fundamental question arose concerning the future of the group. Should they separate, each one going his own way on missions received from the pope, or was it preferable to remain united, in a structured group, "to be so joined and united into one body that no physical separation of our persons, be it ever so great could divide our hearts"?[1] There was no evident solution. Reasons in favor of the maximal mobility required by the mission seemed to recommend a total independence from one another. On the other hand, the friendship which, for years, had united French, Spaniards, Savoyards, Portuguese, and Cantabrians, around the same ideal and the same project, seemed to them to be a gift from God which should be guarded at any price. What would Our Lord want? For three months, from mid-Lent to the feast of John the Baptist, 1539, the companions deliberated this without, however, interrupting their usual ministries. Opinions were divided. Relying on prayer and meditation, and offering penances, they decided to trust in the Lord, certain that they would be enlightened. Every evening, they shared their ideas and as they heard arguments on both sides, their reflection progressed:

> Since our most merciful and affectionate Lord had seen fit to assemble and bind us together—we who are so frail and from such diverse national and cultural backgrounds—we could not sever what God has united and bound together. Rather, with each passing day we ought to confirm

and strengthen ourselves into a single body. Each should have a knowledge
of and a concern for the others, leading to a richer harvest of souls . . . .[2]

A more difficult question remained to be resolved. Should this group,
which they decided to create, take the form of a religious order, which implied
obedience to a superior? Not having any clarity on this, the companions intensified their penance and prayers. Arguments against founding an order were
not lacking. Religious orders were decadent and had a bad reputation among
the people. Obedience was hardly popular, and risked discouraging vocations.
And what if the pope compelled them to submit to a rule which would alter
their original project? A favorable argument was decisive: an order would
assure the continuity and future of the group.

> Finally, with the help of God, we came to a decision. We concluded, not
> only by a majority vote but indeed without a dissenting voice, that it would
> be more advantageous and even essential for us to vow obedience to one
> of our number in order to attain three aims: first, that we might better
> and more exactly pursue our supreme goal of fulfilling the divine will in
> all things; second, that the Society might be more securely preserved; and
> finally, that proper provision might be made for those individual matters,
> of both spiritual and temporal moment, that will arise.[3]

Once the decision was made, each one committed himself to become a
member of the Society when it was approved by the pope. Meanwhile, the
essential traits of the future order had to be made clear. Five brief paragraphs,
drafted by Ignatius and consigned by the companions then present in Rome, set
out the goal, the means, and the structure of the proposed new order.

The pope's approbation was not easy to obtain. The project was not lacking
in originality. In fact, it was innovative as it broke with tradition. The new
order retained few of the traditional characteristics of religious life, e.g., a convent or monastery as the basic domicile, a religious habit, divine office in choir,

and communal penitential practices. To justify this originality, Nadal would later explain "We are priests and not monks."[4] By renouncing everything that might hamper their mobility, the Jesuits wanted to be more available for the missions entrusted to them:

> Our life-style is to live as Christ, the Christian life; if our life appears common exteriorly, it must be noted, however, that interiorly we should tend towards perfection. [. . .] This type of common life seems to us to be the most adaptable above all in our relations with other persons whom we hope to win over for Christ. Persons would avoid us and refuse our friendship if they saw us as persons set apart in what concerns clothing, food, etc.; similarity gives birth to friendship and familiarity whereas dissimilarity drives them away.[5]

If the pope accepted the project favorably, the curial canonists and some influential cardinals were strongly opposed. Their major argument? Rather than found a new religious order, they believed it more beneficial to reform those already existing. To overcome their resistance, Ignatius took drastic action: he asked for letters of recommendation from all his powerful friends, and had no less than three thousand Masses celebrated to change the minds of his opponents. Finally on September 27, 1540, Pope Paul III approved the foundation of the Society in the Bull *Regimini militantis Ecclesiae* but limited the number of professed to sixty.

It thus became necessary to proceed to the election of the superior and the promulgation of the *Constitutions*. Several companions were already scattered in Italy and Portugal. Those who could, came to Rome; the others sent in their votes. As was expected, Ignatius was elected unanimously—except for his own vote. Believing that he was unworthy of exercising this responsibility, and that he was incapable of governing himself let alone others, he initially refused his election and called for another ballot. It produced the same result. After beating around the bush for several days and after consulting his confessor, he finally accepted out of fear of resisting the Holy Spirit. On April 22, they gathered at the Basilica of Saint Paul Outside The Walls, where Ignatius celebrated the Mass during which they pronounced their vows, one after the other, according to the formula then in use in the Society.

The Constitutions

When the companions decided to form a religious order in 1539, they had defined a series of characteristics: obedience to the pope; teaching Christian doctrine to children; formation of candidates to the Society; length of the mandate of the superior general; the practice of poverty, and the procedure for the admission or refusal of candidates.[6] The companions developed these points into "Five Chapters" or "Summary of the Institute," the fundamental charter of the Society which was reflected in the bulls of Paul III (*Regimini militantis Ecclesiae*, 1540) and Julius III (*Exposcit debitum*, 1550).[7] The companions were scattered by the missions confided to them, and Ignatius remained alone to compose the *Constitutions*. The others had confidence in him and approved in advance whatever seemed best to him. Little by little, certain elements fell into place: poverty, refusal of ecclesiastical dignities, distinction between professed members and spiritual coadjutors, impediments to admission into the Society, and the examination of candidates. Ignatius explained the method he followed: he celebrated Mass every day during which he would present the point he was treating to God, and prayed over it. Often visions confirmed his decisions.[8] Some questions called for longer periods of prayer and reflection. The few pages of his *Spiritual Journal* which have come down to us bear witness to the difficulty and time needed for decisions like those concerning poverty: forty days to decide whether the churches of the Society could benefit from revenues.[9] At this pace there was little progress. Work accelerated in 1547 with the arrival of Juan Alfonso de Polanco as his secretary.[10] Polancio, a hard worker, with a clear and methodical mind, and an excellent organizer, made the task easier. The pace quickened to the point that in 1550 Ignatius was able to convoke professed members available to come to Rome to examine together a first draft of the *Constitutions*. Each commented frankly on a text which several found to be too verbose. Ignatius and Polanco took their comments into consideration in a new definitive version which was distributed in the different provinces. Later, during a crisis, Bobadilla would forget this common discussion, and accuse Ignatius of wanting to redact the *Constitutions* by himself.

Despite the care taken in drawing up the *Constitutions*, Ignatius was convinced that a juridical code did not precede life in order to compel it but rather proceeded from life. Since the Society was founded not by human means but through "the omnipotent hand of Christ, God and our Lord," the interior law of charity and love, written and impressed in hearts by the Holy Spirit, was more decisive than any exterior norm.[11] The *Constitutions,* the fruit of a transparent process, continually evaluated, completed or modified by experience, were sufficiently precise to be able to trace a path, indicate a direction and a spirit. The *Constitutions* were conceived according to the model of the *Exercises*; they are more than a juridical text and they propose an itinerary of discernment regarding the structuration of a group. The *Constitutions* address men spiritually mature, always on the move, swept along by life, and in search of greater service. Faithful to this intuition, Ignatius would die without finishing the *Constitutions*. It would be up to his companions, to those who came afterwards, to complete a task undertaken in common.

Notes

1. "Deliberation," p. 328, num. 3.

2. "Deliberation," pp. 328–29, num. 3.

3. "Deliberation," p. 333, num. 8.

4. *Nadal*, vol. 5, pp. 158, 174.

5. *Nadal*, vol. 5, pp. 57, 60.

6. For the various documents, see *Sancti Ignatii de Loyola Constitutiones Societatis Jesu* (3 vols., Rome: Institutum Historicum Societatis Iesu, 1934–1937), vol. 1.

7. *Constitutiones*, vol. 1, pp. 14–21.

8. *Saint Ignatius's Own Story*, p. 70, nums. 100–101.

9. "Spiritual Diary," in *Saint Ignatius of Loyola. Personal Writings*, ed. and trans. Joseph A. Munitiz, S.J., and

Philip Endean, S.J. (London: Penguin, 1996), pp. 73–74.

10. On the role of Polanco, see J. Carlos Coupeau, S.J., "Juan de Polanco's Role as Secretary of Ignatius of Loyola: 'His Memory and Hands,'" in McCoog, *Ite inflammate omnia*, pp. 109–27; J. Carlos Coupeau, S.J., *From Inspiration to Invention: Rhetoric in the Constitutions of the Society of Jesus* (St. Louis: The Institute of Jesuit Sources, 2010).

11. *Constitutions*, pp. 119–20, num. 134; 331, num. 812.

XV

The Superior in Spite of Himself

Ignatius passed the last eighteen years of his life in Rome (1538–1556).[1] That does not mean that his pilgrimage ended. A desire to help souls would not allow him to rest in peace. When he went off to proclaim the Gospel, everything affected him and became a reason for committing himself to apostolic talks despite his precarious health which often obliged him to stay in bed. In Europe, the political and religious upheavals represented so many challenges to which he tried to respond. On other continents, recently discovered cultures gave rise to new projects. He sent companions to Germany, Italy, Sicily, Portugal, Bohemia, Ireland, France, Belgium, India, Japan, Ethiopia, Brazil. Salmerón, Laínez, Jay, and Peter Canisius (1521–1597) were active at the Council of Trent. He gave precise instructions (more than two hundred) to each, whether missionaries or theologians. His counsels, full of wisdom and finesse, touched upon their spiritual life, their comportment in extremely uncertain situations, their apostolic commitments, or their scientific works. The pope, bishops, kings and princes, and civil authorities all made requests to him and he tried to respond by adapting himself to circumstances, without any *a priori* strategy concocted in secret in his little room. The imposing correspondence which he maintained with the powerful did not lead him to neglect his companions scattered to the four corners of the earth, or simple nuns to whom he provided spiritual assistance. Circa 7000 letters written by him personally or by his secretary remain.

Always passionate for Christ, Ignatius accepted life as it presented itself in and through his many relationships. His ever-vigilant creativity gives rise to important new works. Even though he had never dreamed of this previously, he founded and multiplied colleges.[2] By installing the *modus parisiensis* that is the course of studies (liberal arts, philosophy, and theology) as practiced at the University of Paris, he made a powerful contribution to pedagogical renewal first in Europe then abroad. Confronted with the religious conflicts in Europe, with delinquent clergy, and the papal court, Ignatius did not waste time moaning over the sorry state of the Church or denouncing its errors and vices. He acted boldly, without being intimidated by his precarious means, whether of men or of money. In Rome, the Roman College (the future Gregorian University) became an important center for the formation of clergy. In order to remedy the deficient intellectual and spiritual formation of the priests of Central Europe and to contribute usefully to the reform of the clergy caught up in the Lutheran turbulence, he founded the German College at Rome which would become a perpetual financial headache.

Although Ignatius may not have fully realized the consequences for the Society itself of undertaking schools for laymen, in so doing he made a decision that had a transforming impact on the culture of the order. Unlike members of other orders up to that time, Jesuits now had to be proficient not only in the clerical subjects of philosophy and theology, but also in subjects like literature, theatre, astronomy, physics, and mathematics. As a result of Ignatius's decision, Jesuits became poets, theatrical entrepreneurs, experts on the history and theory of dance, engineers, and master cartographers.

Meanwhile, the Society was evolving in other ways. Sent by the pope or requested by bishops and sovereigns, the companions find themselves confronted with new challenges posed by the Protestant Reformation. In addition to the administrative task of governing the Society, Ignatius was solicitous about the state of Catholicism in regions most directly affected. Being very well informed, he intervened with kings and princes.

On September 24, 1549, he gave precise instructions to the companions departing for Germany: let them be kind to everyone; let them make themselves loved even by their adversaries; let no one leave their presence feeling sad; let them speak with competence, avoiding scholastic terminology which did not have a good press; and when they defended the Holy See, let them beware of being dismissed as papalists.[3]

In France, the situation was more delicate. Ignatius had dreams of establishing a center of studies in Paris as he had done in Rome.[4] Even though he had the protection of Charles de Guise (1524–1574). the cardinal of Lorraine, and Guillaume du Prat (1507–1560), Bishop of Clermont, and even though King Henry II (1519–1559) had given his approval first verbally and later in writing, Parlement refused juridical recognition to the Society. By a decree of December 1, 1554, the Faculty of Theology of Paris denied the requested naturalization on the pretext that the Jesuits represented a danger to faith and to the Church. Ignatius did not lose any sleep over this. Refusing to be drawn into a polemic with the Sorbonne, he had recourse to a tactic which had worked for him many times in the past: he solicited recommendations in favor of the Society from princes, governors, magistrates, civil and ecclesiastical authorities, and universities where the Jesuits were working. A meeting at Rome between four of the principle doctors of Paris, among whom was the author of the decree, the Dominican Jean Benoît, a relentless enemy of the Jesuits, and four theologians from the Society, gave a more objective evaluation to the Parisians without obliging the Sorbonne to rescind its decision. The narrow-mindedness of the Gallicans, the prejudices against the Society and the haughty assurance of the doctors however won over reason. It would be necessary to wait until the Colloquy of Poissy between the Huguenots and Catholics, in which Laínez was involved, for the act of naturalization to be signed on September 15, 1561—five years after the death of Ignatius.[5]

The number of Jesuits continued to grow: it was now a far cry from the small group whose relations were spontaneous, amicable and quasi-permanent. In order to maintain the cohesion of this expanding community, Ignatius organized a system of epistolary communication which was meticulously regulated. Each Jesuit should regularly send news of his ministry to Rome, in which he mentioned only edifying events, since these letters would be read by others.

News regarding health and other personal and controversial items should be sent in a supplementary letter, more confidential and spontaneous. Ignatius himself or his secretary answered each. He told one of his correspondents that in a single night he sent off 250 letters, and the archives of the Society conserve a thousand letters just for the year 1555.[6]

For important decisions, Ignatius consulted several Jesuits who formed a group of advisors; they met systematically every day after dinner. The goal being sought, the means to attain it, the advantages and disadvantages of each solution were all carefully examined. Each one had his turn to speak and present his arguments. True discernment took time. In case of doubt, there was no hurry: they would sleep on it and the subject would be taken up again the next day until a satisfactory solution was found. Once the decision is taken, its execution is "as sure and constant as a nail well driven in."[7] There was nothing more to do than to obey unless valid reasons called for another approach. While he was intractable on obedience, Ignatius then handed over the subject's discernment to the one on the scene. As adamant as he might have been when it was question of obedience, Ignatius confided in the discernment of the Jesuit *in situ*. Did he not once say: "I very much want everyone to have an overall indifference, etc., but even so, provided there is obedience and abnegation on the part of the subject, I have found it a great advantage to follow his inclinations"?[8]

"Dictator of His Order, Idol of His Subjects"

The above phrase comes from Pope Paul IV who not only did not like Ignatius personally, but never missed an opportunity to manifest his dislike. Such a view of Ignatius's governance was first suggested to the pope by the boisterous Bobadilla who, after the death of Ignatius, never ceased to settle his scores with the other companions.[9]

Testimonies of most of his companions concerning Ignatius's manner of governing contradict this not very flattering judgement. Ignatius had confidence in his men in so far as they were free of every "disordered affection," and he took into consideration the particular circumstances in which they found themselves. His decisions were the fruit of much reflection and of meticulous discernment. The decision once taken was however never absolute to the point of negating the responsibility of his subjects. To be sure, Ignatius could be intransigent with Jesuits too self-absorbed without the desired apostolic flexibility but, ordinarily, he never imposed more than a Jesuit could support. He was very aware that the Holy Spirit also dwelt in the hearts of his brethren and inspired them. Thus he had more confidence in their docility to follow the interior law of the Spirit rather than to follow the letter of the *Constitutions*. As precise as they might be, the articles of the *Constitutions* were repeatedly accompanied by a referral to the inspiration of the Holy Spirit and to the capacity of discernment on the part of the Jesuit involved.[10]

At Rome, in addition to his preoccupation with the universal Society, Ignatius practically ran the life of the community, and intervened in the formation of candidates. If we are to believe the chronicle of Gonçalves da Câmara, an unconditional admirer, he treated his "inferiors" with circumspection, praising their good points without disclosing their weaknesses. He was intuitive and quickly grasped the needs and expectations of people. As much as possible he did not do any violence to anyone and accommodated himself to the tastes and mood of his companions even in the ordinary details of daily life. He chatted freely with new arrivals, visited them in their room, and invited them to his table; he worried about their acclimation to Rome; he took them out in the morning, before sunrise, to get exercise and breathe good fresh air "so that the local climate, which is harmful to foreigners, should not harm them." In spite of financial difficulties, he purchased a country house so that they could get some healthy air. He took care that the sick were well tended and fittingly nourished; he worried about their comfort, went to make their bed, helped them delouse and get rid of the bedbugs. He had no qualms about selling the house's pewter-ware to buy them blankets. He was attentive and patient with those who were tempted. He watched out for the novices, taught them to know themselves and to develop their natural qualities for the Lord's service. He moderated their zeal to do penance and dispensed the weakest from fasting.[11] When Nadal worried about the scandal this dispensation could provoke, he replied that if someone of the household was scandalized by that, he would be dismissed from the Society at once.[12]

"A tiny, little Spaniard, a bit lame, with joyful eyes"; such was the description of Ignatius by an infatuated admirer from Padua as cited by Laínez.[13] He was certainly small: Ignatius measured 1.67 meters (about 5'5"). He himself told his companions that when he embraced a tall young candidate, he had to jump to put his arms around his neck.[14] As for joyful eyes, a witness remarked that, because of so many tears, he eyes were usually so tired that they looked like the eyes of a dead man. His face radiated peace and serenity, which remained unaltered, come what may, whether he received good news or bad. His personality exercised a sort of fascination on all who came into contact with him; nobody remained insensitive to what he said. At home, he established a rather familiar and relaxed atmosphere. He was always amiable, master of himself, and detested outbursts and everything that betrayed excitement. He exacted silence, especially at times of prayer, liked cleanliness and order, politeness and discipline. He was affable without being familiar, always having a friendly word of encouragement for those whom he met. He spoke well of everyone, and never mentioned the faults of others, even if they were generally known. His confidence in God, his peace and a restrained interior joy were contagious. A mysterious power and a divine light seemed to shine forth from his person. Those who encountered him found themselves strengthened in their vocation. This was how his admirers and most of his companions perceived him.

A good part of these edifying traits are related by Gonçalves da Câmara, who every now and then tends to mythologize the founder.[15] A simple reading of the Prologue of his *Memorial* shows clearly that his admiration for Ignatius prompted him to idealize everything done and said by one "whom our Lord gave us as an example and head of this mystical body, of which all sons of the

Society."[16] Not everyone shared this opinion, including some companions who were cofounders. Simão Rodrigues, who was, to be sure, in crisis, accused him of being "a father who loved his son more in words than in deeds and whose severity stirred up revolt and anger." Nicolás Bobadilla, in a memorial sent to Pope Paul IV, reproached Ignatius for wanting to draw up the *Constitutions* by himself "because he was a despotic father and manager who only did whatever came into his head."[17]

While he was full of kindness towards the weak, he could be severe with those whom he believed to be spiritually strong, and his fits of anger made the house tremble. He was very exacting, even without consideration, with his most trusted men. Under the pretext of giving them hard bread, a manly food, he inflicted remarkably harsh penances for trivialities. Laínez, Nadal and Polanco personally suffered such painful incidences that they nearly shed tears. Because of his persistence in a certain manner, Laínez was told: "All right, you take charge of the Society, you govern it!"[18] This reaction took his breath away.[19] On another day, he asked God: "What have I done against the Society to make this holy man treat me the way he does?"[20] In his *Memorial*, Gonçalves da Câmara went to great lengths to excuse these harsh character traits and added, with some exaggeration: "There was no one in the Society who did not love him greatly, and did not himself think that the Father loved him very dearly."[21] As for Ribadeneira, he had no qualms about spinning these fits of anger as acts of virtue even though he simultaneously tried to persuade the Jesuit superiors not to imitate the founder in this regard.[22] In the writings of his admirers, the statue of the founder remains intact: Ignatius is the perfect superior, always master of himself, who has no intention other than the spiritual progress of his companions.

There was a mixture of kindness and inflexibility in Ignatius. Sometimes he could be rigid and demanding, sometimes amiable and understanding—even maternal—with those who were suffering. He showed that he could be accommodating by adjusting himself to the needs of his companions or he could be merciless and intolerant in the face of certain faults. For lapses in modesty—not very seriously, so it seemed—he had Jesuits thrown out of the Society in the middle of the night and against the advice of his counselors.[23] Did the behavior he censured stir up ill-digested memories of his unbridled youth?

Ignatius was certainly a charismatic superior. In the opinion of all who had contact with him, the portrait of the superior general as delineated in the ninth section of the *Constitutions* was very much his own.[24] He had qualities which attracted and reassured. At the beginning his first followers, then those of the second generation, were in some way captivated by a personality who incarnated the ideals which haunted them and which found their expression in him. They recognized themselves in the project of the founder. This identification gave them the strength to accept the demands, and the sometimes rude authority, of the one with whom they shared a same absolute aim: the following of Christ. Later, as the Society increased, persons with a less tried or more fragile character would oblige the founder to recognize that not every Jesuit was necessarily cut out to be a hero. Some would leave the Society voluntarily; others would be dismissed. Although he would have wished to prolong the amical style that characterized the early years, different crises contributed to a hardening of his attitude in contentious cases.

THE TASTE OF POWER

Ignatius was at ease with people of power—popes, bishops, emperors, kings, princes, and other wielders of authority. His origin and education at the court had prepared him to interact with the powerful of this world, and his independent character preserved him from any sort of servile attitude. The apostolic zeal, which led him to strive for the greatest good, made him particularly attentive to people who, by their position and instruction, had the most influence.[25] But he certainly did not try to make a place for himself in the courts of the mighty. Quite the contrary. The Biscayan noble who, on the outskirts of Montserrat, had exchanged his clothes with those of a poor devil, never looked back. The acceptance, even the desire for poverty, opprobrium and humiliations to the point of being regarded as deranged and foolish for Christ, were part of his fundamental option.[26] It was along this path that he wanted the candidates to the Society to walk.[27]

When, in the *Constitutions,* he treated the maintenance of a good spirit within the Society, he excluded the ambition of power, "the mother of all the evils in any community or congregation whatsoever."[28] Any direct or indirect pursuit of a dignity or prelature within the Society was forbidden; a Jesuit should not follow an ecclesiastical career and those who did, should be denounced. He himself, as we have seen, had a great deal of difficulty in accepting his election as superior general. In 1551, in a note transmitted to the companions in Rome to study a first draft of the *Constitutions*, he informed them of his renunciation:

> Upon examining the matter factually and, so far as I could perceive within myself, without any emotional bias, I have come on many and varied occasions to the factual conclusion that because of my many sins, many imperfections, and many inward and outward infirmities, I lack to an almost infinite degree the qualities required for the responsibility over the Society which I presently hold by the Society's appointment and imposition.
>
> I desire in our Lord that this matter be carefully examined, and that another person be elected who can carry out my present office of governing the Society better, or less poorly, than I.[29]

Even if his health had notably deteriorated, this pathetic appeal was not simply the result of fatigue. He had thought about it for months, even years; it was a debate within his conscience.

This man cannot be accused of being ambitious, of being someone who, with an iron will, organized and dominated life as a result of his appetite for power. It is true that he had a passionate temperament, was possessed by a very high ideal of following Christ, and of the total gift which this demanded.

Accustomed to giving orders, he was authoritarian but certainly not a person who thirsted after power. Even if they were not without some foundation, the accusations launched by Rodrigues and Bobadilla, both companions who were in crisis, and relayed by the irascible Pope Paul IV, belong more to the category of calumny.

The Obedience of a Corpse

The authoritarianism of Ignatius, his idea of obedience, and his fits of anger all pose the same question. In a directive that Polanco was ordered to write to the companions of the house in Rome, Ignatius demanded that whenever a superior called, a Jesuit should come immediately, interrupting any activity, for obedience to the superior had priority over any other task. Someone in the middle of hearing confession or administering urgent medical assistance should ask the superior if he could finish the task before responding to his call![30] In the *Constitutions,* Ignatius expressed the same opinion: it was a question of obeying like a corpse which lets itself be taken anywhere at all and treated in any which way.[31] The author of the order was Christ, the superior, simply his lieutenant; what was at stake was the Kingdom of God. Such imperatives left no room for delay. When confronted with the Portuguese Jesuits whose obedience left something to be desired, Ignatius gave proof of an extreme intransigence. He instructed their provincial to do one of two things: either throw them out of the Society, or send them to Rome where he would personally handle the matter. The letter was accompanied by decrees of expulsion which only needed a signature.[32] If the temperament of the former Basque captain partly explained this extreme rigor, an experience of another order provided a more mystical justification. In the chapel of La Storta, Ignatius saw the Father putting him with the Son who was carrying the cross and he heard the Son say to him: "I want you to serve us." Such an enlistment did not brook any delay, at any moment, for him or for every other Jesuit.[33]

In the letter on obedience addressed to the Portuguese Jesuits, Ignatius clearly stated that he wanted Jesuits to distinguish themselves among religious orders by the practice of a perfect obedience. They should not be satisfied with a voluntarist submission, with pure execution, but try to make the judgement of the superior their own without seeking to influence him to order what they desire.[34]

Ignatius was certainly not a petty self-important superior, a martinet, as some have depicted him. Obedience, such as he envisaged it, had nothing to do with barrack life. It was situated within the context of discernment, of seeking God's will. It guaranteed the availability and mobility of the Jesuit, the criteria of the freedom of someone ready to commit himself to any mission entrusted to him. Because the government of the Society is a "spiritual government," obedience presupposed a dialogue rooted in trust between the superior and his subject, an authentic opening of the conscience. On the part of the subject, this implied an obligation to represent his point of view and his arguments in favor of his resolution, as long as the final decision remained the prerogative of the superior. If Ignatius did not tolerate those who only did whatever came into their head, he was ready to follow the suggestions of those who had proved their obedience and abnegation.[35]

Ribadeneira related a charming episode. Some young Jesuits were doing excavation work in the gardens of the major Roman house that was alongside a busy street. A novice of noble descent was so ashamed of being seen doing this servile work by any passersby that he considered leaving the Society. Ignatius noticed his discomfort and spoke to the Jesuit who was in charge of the group:

> Do not you know that this novice is tempted to leave because of this job? Why did you summon him to do it? You gave me the order to send everyone, without exception, to do this job. Even if I gave this order, as the person in charge should you not have shown a bit of discernment?

He called the novice and dispensed him from the job.[36] When Olivier Mannaerts (1523–1614), rector of the college in Loreto, asked him what rule should be applied in a specific case, Ignatius replied: "Do as you see best and as the unction [of the Spirit] will guide you; adapt the rules to the situations as best you can." And concerning some delicate nominations to positions of responsibility, Ignatius said: "Olivier, fashion the vestments out of the material you have at your disposal." When this same Olivier confessed to having acted contrary to an express order that he had been given, Ignatius said: "Man gives orders, but God gives discernment. In the future, I want you to act without scruples, taking the circumstances into account, in spite of rules and orders."[37]

He himself did not show good judgement the day he blindly and meekly obeyed an inexperienced doctor whose remedies brought him to death's door.[38] Gonçalves da Câmara, who related this story, did not hesitate to portray Ignatius as the model of perfect obedience, all the while recognizing that he behaved like someone who had lost his mind.[39] He forgot that the founder had inscribed in the *Constitutions* that it was necessary to be reasonable and that everyone should speak to the superior whenever he noticed something harmful to his health.

His obedience to the pope and to the bishops has perhaps been idealized by his admirers who trivialized his spirit of independence and presented his efforts to impose his projects as acts of virtue. When commands of authorities impeded plans which, in his eyes, reflected the will of God, he resisted. When the Franciscan provincial refused him a residence permit, he only yielded when threatened with excommunication. In order to escape the orders of the Inquisition, he successively left Alcalá and Salamanca. When the canon lawyers of the Roman curia raised serious objections about the foundation of the Society, he implemented a strategy to advance his project despite all the opposition. When the popes tried to nominate certain Jesuits as bishops or cardinals, he moved heaven and earth to thwart these initiatives. Would he, therefore, align himself with those whom he denounced in the *Exercises,*[40] because they manipulated things so that God would do what they wanted him to do? Meissner prefers to think that the tension between his behavior and his concept of obedience reflected non-resolved conflictual authoritarian aspects of his own personality.[41]

Notes

1. On Ignatius as administrator, see Markus Friedrich, "Ignatius's Governing and Administering the Society of Jesus," in Maryks, *Companion*, pp. 123–40.

2. On Jesuit education, see the "Introduction" to *Jesuit Pedagogy, 1540–1616*, eds. Cristiano Casalini and Claude Pavur, S.J. (Chestnut Hill, Mass.: Institute of Jesuit Sources, 2016), pp. 1–33; *The Jesuit Ratio Studiorum*, ed. Vincent J. Duminuco, S.J. (New York: Fordham University Press, 2000); Paul F. Grendler, "Jesuit Schools in Europe: A Historiographical Essay," *Journal of Jesuit Studies* 1 (2014), pp. 7–25.

3. *Letters and Instructions*, pp. 291–97.

4. See García-Villoslada, *San Ignacio de Loyola*, pp. 773–74.

5. On the difficulties in France, see Philippe Lécrivain, S.J., "The Struggle for Paris: Juan Maldonado In France," in *The Mercurian Project. Forming Jesuit Culture, 1573–1580*, ed. Thomas M. McCoog, S.J. (Rome/St. Louis: Institutum Historicum Societatis Iesu/ The Institute of Jesuit Sources, 2004), pp. 295–321.

6. See Pierre Emonet, S.J., "Amis dans le Seigneur. La correspondence entre Ignace, Pierre Favre et Francois Xavier," *Christus* 209 (January, 2006), pp. 100–109.

7. *Remembering Íñigo*, p. 14, num. 20.

8. *Remembering Íñigo*, p. 72, num. 117.

9. For a distinctly anti-Bobadilla interpretation of these conflicts, see Bangert, *Jerome Nadal*, pp. 171–92.

10. *Constitutions*, pp. 119–20, 130, 204, 277–78, nums. 134, 161, 414, 624. On this "negotiated obedience," see Silvia Mostaccio, *Early Modern Jesuits between Obedience and Conscience during the Generalate of Claudio Acquaviva (1581–1615)* (Farnham: Ashgate, 2014).

11. *Remembering Íñigo*, pp. 21–22, 65–66, 68–69, nums. 31, 109, 114.

12. *Nadal*, vol. 1, p. 24.

13. *Remembering Íñigo*, p. 109, num. 180.

14. *Remembering Íñigo*, p. 31, num. 47.

15. Cacho Nazabal, *Ignacio de Loyola*, pp. 381–90.

16. *Remembering Íñigo*, p. 4, num. 3.

17. *Nadal*, vol. 4, p. 733.

18. *Fontes narrativi*, vol. 1, pp. 587–588.

19. *Nadal*, vol. 4, pp. 102, 104.

20. *Fontes narrativi*, vol. 3, pp. 620–21.

21. *Remembering Íñigo*, p. 53, num. 84.

22. *Fontes narrativi*, vol. 3, pp. 620–21.

23. *Remembering Íñigo*, p. 37, num. 56.

24. *Constitutions*, pp. 309–11, nums. 723–35.

25. *Constitutions*, pp. 274–75, num. 622.

26. *Spiritual Exercises*, pp. 61–62, 69, nums. 146–47, 167.

27. "General Examen," in *Constitutions*, pp. 106–109, nums. 98–103.

28. *Constitutions*, p. 334, num. 817.

29. Ignatius to Members of the Society of Jesus, Rome, 30 January 1551, *Letters and Instructions*, pp. 329–30.

30. Ignatius to Jesuits at the house in Rome, Rome, 24 August 1550, *Letters and Instructions*, pp. 320–21.

31. *Constitutions*, pp. 247–48, num. 547.

32. Ignatius to Diero Mirón, Rome, 17 December 1552, *Letters and Instructions*, pp.402–404.

33. See Christopher van Ginhoven Rey, "The Jesuit Instrument: On Saint Ignatius of Loyola's Modernity," in Maryks, *Companion*, pp. 198–215.

34. Ignatius to Fall Members of the Society in Portugal, Rome, 26 March 1553, *Letters and Instructions*, pp. 412–23.

35. *Remembering Íñigo*, p. 72, num. 117.

36. *Fontes narrativi*, vol. 2, p. 482.

37. *Fontes narrativi*, vol. 3, p. 434.

38. *Fontes narrativi*, vol. 1, pp. 547–48.

39. *Remembering Íñigo*, pp. 23–24, num. 35.

40. *Spiritual Exercises*, pp. 64–65, num. 154.

41. *Ignatius of Loyola*, pp. 229–37.

XVI

Friendship Put to the Test

In 1537, in a letter written in Venice, Ignatius announced the arrival of "nine friends of mine in the Lord [. . .] four of them Spaniards, two Frenchmen, two from Savoy, and one from Portugal."[1] Although they were unanimous regarding their project, the friends were aware from the start that differences could threaten the cohesion of their group. Some came from countries at war with one another; some, such as Ignatius, Francis Xavier and Rodrigues, came from noble families, while others, such as Favre, Bobadilla and Salmerón were from more humble origins. Laínez was a "New Christian," descended from converted Jews and objects of suspicion in 16th-century Spain.

The important missions entrusted to them by the pope, their earned confidence of sovereigns and elites, the importance of their tasks and ministries, their maneuverability and availability, their strong personalities at times intoxicated by success, all menaced the group's unity. To maintain internal coherence Ignatius relied primarily on the obedience characteristic of the Society, on the manifestation of conscience with superiors, and on an exchange of information. This did not prevent certain conflicts among them and sometimes serious ones.

Rodrigues, a Painful and Complicated Case

At the request of King John III (1502–1557), Simão Rodrigues had returned to his native Portugal with the intention of embarking for the Indies with Francis Xavier. Awaiting their departure, the two companions worked so well that the king wanted to keep them in Portugal. Xavier, however, left, but Rodrigues remained to establish the Society within the kingdom. His holiness, profound spirituality, and apostolic zeal earned him the admiration of the court, of the clergy, and of the people. He also attracted so many candidates to the Society that, two years later, he could establish a college at Coimbra, the intellectual capital of the country. Ignatius, who had absolute confidence in him, appointed him provincial of Portugal in 1546, the first provincial of the first province in the Society. But certain reservations and even criticisms of his style of governance reached Rome: Rodrigues tolerated excessive penitential practices among the Jesuit scholastics, prayers and preaching which were not in the style of the still young Society, "real follies," according to Martín de Santa Cruz, rector of the college at Coimbra.[2]

To clarify the situation, Ignatius invited Simão to Rome. The king, shrewdly intervened, opposed his departure, and Ignatius backed down. Soon Ignatius was accused of persecuting Simão, and the province was divided between partisans of Simão (the "simonists") and those of Ignatius.[3] A Jesuit confidant of Simão, Miguel Gomes, spread calumnies against Ignatius in the court where they fell upon complacent ears: he only looked out for his own interests; he ran the Society as if he owned it; he wanted to divert money from Portugal to Rome; he was ambitious and worldly, and wanted to marry his niece to the son of Francis Borja, Duke of Gandía.[4] Simão even talked of making Portugal independent of Rome. Meanwhile, Ignatius bided his time while still inviting Simão to visit Rome with the other cofounders to examine a first draft of the *Constitutions*. After several postponements, Simão finally presented himself to Ignatius who received him fraternally and affectionately. Simão explained his side of the story and apologized for past errors. But once back in Portugal, he again bitterly criticized Ignatius.

On December 27, 1551, Ignatius, now convinced that Simão was incapable of restoring order in the province, officially relieved him from the burdens of office with concerns about his health offered as grounds for the removal. Five days later without any mention of Rodrigues's health, Ignatius named him provincial of Aragon. Simão initially refused the nomination and then stalled for a time by taking refuge in the home of a friend João de Lencastre, Duke of Aveiro (1501–1571), until threats of expulsion from the Society prompted a change of mind and he capitulated. But he only remained a few months in his new province. He disliked everything about it: food, climate, dialect. Requests to return to Portugal were finally heeded, and Ignatius sent him to the community of San Fins. Portuguese superiors, unaware of this permission, refused to receive him. Once again, Simão took refuge with the duke.

In 1552, Ignatius tried to defuse the situation by sending an emissary to Portugal, Miguel de Torres (1509–1593), who took drastic measures to resolve the conflict: between 90 and 130 Jesuits were dismissed from the Society. The following year, Jerónimo Nadal visited the province as a commissioner with full powers to promulgate the *Constitutions*. Finally, that same year, Francis Borja, admired and venerated by all with strong contacts at the Portuguese court, tried to reestablish peace and morale.

Faced with a situation that had become an impasse, Ignatius summoned Rodrigues to Rome: "My son, Master Simão, have confidence in me in everything." At the same time, in case Rodrigues did not comply, Ignatius sent an unsigned order of expulsion, dated June 24, 1553, to the Portuguese provincial Diego Mirón (1516–1590) But Simão was in no hurry until Mirón, fixed a definite date for his departure on pain of excommunication. He left for Rome reluctantly while affirming that he would soon return to Portugal since he was thoroughly convinced that, without him, the Society was in danger of perishing. At Rome, Ignatius again received him with love. Simão bitterly complained of his treatment and asked that a commission decide his case. Four judges were thus appointed. After studying the case for several months, they judged that, for the good of the Society, Simão Rodrigues should not return to Portugal. They reproached him for being too attached to his native land, for having an excessive concern for his comfort, and for presumptuous ambition and pride. The judges even proposed a severe penance, but Ignatius annulled that punishment immediately.

In his immediate reaction, Rodrigues no longer wanted to live within the Society but as a hermit. After a brief attempt, he travelled around Italy, never at ease, never finding a place that suited him. Ignatius paid all his expenses, and dispensed him from the customary rules regarding fast and abstinence. Still bitter, Simão openly criticized him, alleging that Ignatius did not respect him. He replied to his former friend's amiable letters with words reeking of cynicism.

This conflict troubled Ignatius more than any attack from external enemies. It touched the very core of a Jesuit's vocation. By refusing obedience and denouncing mobility, a companion (or cofounder) personified the rejection of the ideal Ignatius desired with the formation of the Society of Jesus. The attitude of his friend, the provincial of Portugal, meant the failure of his own project. It is easier to understand the radicalism of his conception of obedience as expressed in his letter to the Jesuits of Portugal when the crisis was at its height.

Rodrigues was undoubtedly an unstable personality with a temperament subject to depression. To be fair to him, it must be acknowledged that Ignatius had a hard time managing this crisis. By intervening from Rome, without being on the scene, he certainly committed several errors. The people he sent to resolve the problems on the spot were not the most suitable, and they only succeeded in making Rodrigues dig in his heels a bit more. The provincial Mirón, a hesitant person, lacked flexibility. The emissary, Miguel Torres, was authoritarian; his methods shocked the hypersensitive temperament of Rodrigues. Only Francis Borja, sent as a last resort, showed himself to be more conciliatory by proposing practical solutions which took into account the susceptibility and pride of Rodrigues. But it was too late. Torn between respect for the person and the common good of the Society, Ignatius had trouble finding the right words and gave the impression of wanting to have it both ways. The same day that he addressed to Rodrigues letters overflowing with kind words, understanding and confidence, he was writing severe and forceful letters, along with decrees of expulsion, to his superiors. It was easy for Simão to accuse him of duplicity and to sketch a very negative portrait of Ignatius which would subsequently become fodder for a dark legend.[5]

Bobadilla, an Impulsive, Difficult Colleague

The case of Bobadilla, although less complicated, was, nonetheless, another hard blow for Ignatius and the other companions. Nicolás Alonso, born in Bobadilla del Camino, was intelligent, lively, sometimes showing sparks of genius, very sociable, particularly gifted at building up relationships. Capable of living in hospices as well as in palaces, of mixing with nobility as well as with simple people, he could feast and drink to the point of losing control of himself. He had a spontaneous temperament, excessive and rather unrestrained, very independent and easily satisfied with himself; diplomacy was certainly not his principle virtue. He especially liked to do battle with the Lutherans. His criticisms of the *Interim* of Augsburg of 1548, specifically some temporary concessions made to Lutherans by Emperor Charles V until a future council could resolve them definitively, divided the court and angered the emperor who had him escorted to the border of the empire. Bobadilla's lack of prudence irritated Ignatius who consequently took his time before readmitting him into the community. Several years later, Bobadilla again publically criticized the *Interim* and a mentality that eventually produced the famous formula "He who rules, his is the religion"(*cuius regio, eius religio*).

By his independence, Bobadilla stood out among the first companions. Although he accepted and signed the *Deliberation* of 1539, he would later pugnaciously defend a system of collegial government. The affairs of the Society did not seem to interest him. When Ignatius invited him to Rome for the election of the first superior general, he refused to come and his vote never arrived at the curia. He did not show any interest in promulgating the *Constitutions* and refused to approve the requirements prior to solemn profession, among which was a period teaching catechism to children. On several occasions, the minutes of the group's deliberations mention that all except Bobadilla approved such and such a decision. Soon his recurring objections would oblige the companions to rule that decisions would henceforth be made by majority vote and no longer unanimously. Nadal explained: "So it was decided that, if one member of the group had an opinion contrary to the others, he would not be allowed to treat other matters. This is the reason why in the early records no mention is made of Bobadilla."[6]

During the lifetime of Ignatius, Bobadilla led an independent life, without concerning himself too much about the rest of the Society. He felt as though he was neither recognized nor appreciated by those who govern it. Friendships with the elites and his own apostolic successes went to his head. It is true that the pope, bishops and princes entrusted him with numerous and prestigious missions while his lack of prudence alienated him from his colleagues. He would have liked to have exercised offices within the Society, but they were always refused to him. "In the milieus of the Church and at the Court he felt like a prince. In the milieus of the Society and its curia he felt like a buffoon."[7] When Ignatius reproached him for not writing regularly to Rome to give news of himself or not submitting the conventional forms, he casually replied that he had other things to do. But he was not too busy to refrain from criticizing certain expressions of Ignatius, from pointing out imprecisions in his vocabulary, or from correcting a mistaken address. Ignatius accepted these remarks in a conciliatory spirit: "As for your not deigning to read my letters for lack of time: by the grace of God I have more than enough time and inclination to read and reread all of yours."[8]

It is above all after the death of Ignatius that Bobadilla would go over the edge with bitter criticisms against the founder's style of governance. Since he was a friend of Pope Paul IV, his criticisms found a sympathetic hearer in the pontiff. He wrote that Ignatius was "certainly a prudent person, but someone who clung to his views, as your Holiness knows all too well. What is good in him should be recognized, but his defects cannot be defended at all costs."[9] What were Ignatius's defects? That he governed like an absolute despot who only did whatever passed through his head, and that the *Constitutions* contained items contrary to the Holy

See. As the Society searched for a successor to Ignatius, Bobadilla would urge the pope to take things into hand and to call the professed members to Rome to review the *Constitutions*, and to invite the Faculty of Theology at the Sorbonne to present its criticism of the Society. He argued that the government of the Society should be collegial and under the administration of the founding Fathers. Thus he had a grudge against the three Jesuits who prepared the General Congregation: Laínez, Polanco and Nadal, whom he described as "three monkeys [. . .] three indiscreet, passionate and ambitious little kids [. . .] who took themselves for the whole Society."[10] He himself was even ready to assume the government of the Society if it were offered to him.[11] Nadal, who had no sympathy for him, reproached him as being a seditious person "who, by his words and his writings denounced the Society to the Sovereign Pontiff [. . .] who would destroy it, if he could."[12] And elsewhere, Nadal wrote: "We were so ingenious that we never would have imagined that one of our own would dare to attack the Society until Bobadilla's maneuvers were discovered."[13]

NOTES

1. Ignatius to Jean de Verdolay, Venice, 24 July 1537, *Letters and Instructions*, pp. 28–31.

2. *Fabri Monumenta . . . Epistolae, Memoriale et Processus* (Madrid: Lopez del Horno, 1914), pp. 198–99, 342–50.

3. Loyola to Pedro de Tablares, Rome, 6 November 1553, *Epistolae et instructiones*, vol. 5, pp, 675–76.

4. Gonçalves da Câmara to Leão Henriques, Lisbon, 15 October 1552, *Epistolae mixtae ex variis Europae locis* (5 vols., Madrid: Lopez del Horno, 1898–1901), vol. 2, pp. 807–08.

5. For more on the problem of Rodrigues, see Bangert, *Jerome Nadal, passim*, and José Vaz de Carvalho, S.J., "The Rehabilitation of Simão Rodrigues, S.J.," in *The Mercurian Project. Forming Jesuit Culture, 1573–1580*, ed. Thomas M. McCoog, S.J. (Rome/St. Louis: Institutum Historicum Societatis Iesu/ The Institute of Jesuit Sources, 2004), pp. 421–35.

6. *Nadal*, vol. 2, p. 52.

7. Cacho Nazabal, *Ignacio de Loyola*, p. 277.

8. Ignatius to Bobadilla, Rome, 1543, *Letters and Instructions*, pp. 94–98.

9. *Nadal*, vol. 4, p. 733.

10. *Nadal*, vol. 4, pp. 106–108, 733.

11. *Nadal*, vol. 4, pp. 104–106.

12. *Nadal*, vol. 4, p. 132.

13. *Nadal*, vol. 2, p. 55.

XVII

Women in the Life of Ignatius

Women played a large role in the life of Ignatius. He loved them but kept his distance. Perhaps it was maternal tenderness which he first sought from them, something of which he had been deprived because of the premature death of his mother. During his youthful follies, he seduced them; in critical moments they helped him; as the Society was being formed, they facilitated the business aspects of his enterprises by providing access to major courts and by generously financing his works. Like a properly brought-up gentleman, he was courteous with them, respected them, and treated them with consideration. Later, he would come to their aid by generously dedicating himself to their spiritual life. Women were sensitive to the strength and tenderness of his personality; they admired him, venerated him, protected him, and helped him without measuring their efforts.

If his relationships with women were frequent, they were sometimes complicated. To begin with, there was his rapport with a mother he hardly knew and of whom he never spoke. According to his wet-nurse, María Garín, it was above all to his sister-in-law, Magdalena de Araoz, wife of his eldest brother Martín, that he owed his first education. It was she who took care of him during his long convalescence at Loyola and passed on to him the books which were at the origin of his conversion. He was susceptible to her charms; years later he would confess that her beauty still troubled him when he contemplated an image of the Madonna whose visage reminded him of his sister-in-law.[1]

During his adolescence and early youth at Arévalo, Ignatius had experienced great sexual freedom which was, however, tempered by a romantic relationship to the woman of his dreams who incarnated the ideal image of femininity. An apparition of Our Lady with the Child Jesus put an end to his erotico-chivalrous fantasies.

At Manresa, it was a woman, Inés Pascual, who escorted him to the hospice and provided his first supper. Once again pious women listened to this strange pilgrim when he spoke of the things of God. They looked out for him, made sure that he did not harm his health too much, and that he dressed warmly. Did he fall sick because of his excesses of austerity? They cared for him and lodged him until he was better. These prolonged relations between him and his feminine entourage became the object of gossip which, in the opinion of some, precipitated his departure from Manresa. At Barcelona, he found Inés Pascual and Isabel Roser, who helped him embark for the Holy Land and who later encouraged him to take up studies. He remained grateful to these friends until his death.

Later, at Alcalá, women gathered in his room to listen and receive the spiritual exercises from him: married women, widows, young ladies of celebrated beauty. They sometimes visited very early in the morning and took hazardous initiatives by undertaking imprudent pilgrimages. Some swooned and there was talk of cases of hysteria. In all this Meissner sees a case of transference.[2] But that was all that was needed for the Inquisition to intervene and to end this suspicious apostolate.

For a long time, malicious insinuations accompanied Ignatius and his companions, all the more so in that they did not live in monasteries or convents, that they did not wear a religious habit, and that they received women in ordinary places. Remember that Melchor Cano and Tomás de Pedroche reproached them for the casualness of their relations with women. At Rome rumors circulated about Francis Xavier and Jean Codure when women whom they were directing spiritually became pregnant. As for Ignatius, he treated women in distress and prostitutes with considerable kindness and did not hesitate to accompany them along streets of Rome without worrying about criticism and malicious gossip. In 1540, the prefect of the Vatican Custom

Bureau, Mathia dalle Poste, denounced the Jesuits to Pope Paul III and accused each of having a few concubines at Casa Santa Marta with whom they did what they wanted.[3] These rumors caused Ignatius to recommend the greatest prudence to his companions and to engage in conversations only with women of "high rank."[4] As if they were less suspicious! But this distinction reflected the times and milieu. An instruction given to the companions sent on mission disclosed how he understood himself vis-à-vis women: "In a general way, he should prescind from the outward person and look upon the creature, not as good-looking or attractive, but as someone bathed in the blood of Christ, an image of God, a temple of the Holy Spirit, etc."[5]

Letters with women of "high rank" comprise a considerable part of his correspondence as Superior General of the Society.[6] Some placed themselves under his direction; almost all used their influence to promote the works of the Society. Queen Catherine of Portugal (1507–1578) helped resolve the grave crisis provoked by the behavior of Simão Rodrigues; Margaret of Parma, future regent of Belgium, collaborated effectively with the foundation of the house of the catechumens and the House of Saint Martha; the difficult Duchess Eleanor of Florence (1522–1562) made him promises she never fulfilled; Leonor de Mascarenhas, the governess of King Philip II (1527–1598), assisted him with alms as much as she could and presented. These certainly useful relationships were not without inconveniences. More than once Ignatius found himself held hostage by these noble ladies, torn between the recognition he owed them by giving them the confessors they clamored for and the Society's needs of men with mobility for the mission.

The case of Princess Juana of Spain (1535–1573), daughter of Charies V and Regent of Spain, was more complex. After the death of her husband, the princess considered the monastic life. Under the influence of Antonio Araoz (1515–1573) and Francis Borja, she decided to become a Jesuit. Faced with the *fait accompli*, Ignatius did not dare refuse but acquiesced without enthusiasm. She was admitted into the Society with the greatest secrecy, and pronounced the vows of a scholastic, vows that the superior general could dispense. This was a prudent measure which left a loophole in the case that the princess, for reasons of state, would want to remarry. The secret was so strict that Ignatius used a masculine pseudonym, Mateo Sanchez, when he referred to odd member of his Society of men in his correspondence. Juana, very knowledgeable politically, but authoritarian and imperious, took up the defense of the Jesuits against their opponents, Melchor Cano and Bishop Siliceo; she effectively supported the foundation of the Roman College and the college in Valladolid as well as the reform of several convents in Spain. If she was a precious support for Ignatius, more than once she complicated his life by imposing her royal will.[7]

Among the women he directed, Sister Teresa Rejadell, a nun of the Benedictine convent of Santa Clara, in Barcelona was the recipient of one of the very beautiful letters of direction which Ignatius wrote—a faithful resume of his concept of the spiritual life and, without doubt, one of the best commentaries of the rules of spiritual discernment put forward in the *Exercises*.[8]

Ignatius also committed himself to the restoration of fervor in communities of consecrated women. Remember his first initiative in Barcelona which ended with his suffering a serious beating. Later on, at the request of certain bishops, he would intervene in the reform of convents of nuns in Catania (Sicily), at Gaeta, at Rome, at Brignoles (Provence), as is attested by the rather precise instructions he gave to the Jesuits entrusted with this ministry.[9] But he nevertheless consistently refused to allow the Society to assume responsibility for convents of religious women. The only articulated motive for this refusal was that the mobility desired of Jesuits prevented them from being bound to a sedentary task. He explained this to Sister Rejadell and her prioress who were insisting that their convent be put under obedience to the Society.

> . . . for, although in our Society, as one of the many obligations which it holds especially dear in our Lord, there is the wholehearted will to console and serve you in conformity with our profession, the authority of the Vicar of Christ has closed the door against our taking on any government or

superintendence of religions, a thing which the Society begged from the beginning. This is because it was judged that it would be for the greater service of God our Lord that we should have as few ties as possible in order to be able to go wherever obedience to the Sovereign Pontiff and the needs of our neighbours may call us.[10]

An unconditional admirer of Ignatius and, moreover, a close friend, would confirm him, in spite of herself, in his decision not to accept a feminine branch of the Society. Isabel Roser belonged to an influential family in Barcelona and had enabled Ignatius to realize several of his dreams, beginning with his trip to the Holy Land. It was also Isabel who, after his return, encouraged him to study and who found him a teacher. Along with a group of women from high society, she sustained him financially during his years of grammar studies in Barcelona and continued to help him in Paris as she followed with interest, the beginnings of the group of companions. Her attachment to Ignatius evidently inspired malevolent commentaries. Having fragile nerves, Isabel experienced all the more difficulty supporting these calumnies in that Ignatius, now studying in Paris, was not replying to her letters. Consolation finally arrived in the form of a very long letter which reassured her: the links of friendship have not relaxed, above all with Isabel "for to you I owe more than to anyone I know in this life."[11]

Fifteen years later, after the death of her husband, Isabel decided to rejoin Ignatius in Rome with other companions, to put themselves under his obedience and to work with him. Antonio Araoz, provincial of Spain, to whom Isabel had revealed her desire, encouraged her while Favre was more skeptical. Ignatius, torn between the immense debt of gratitude which he owed to his benefactor, and his decision not to accept a feminine branch of the Society, stalled for time. He tried, in vain, to reason with Isabel and warned his companions against such dangerous initiatives. Nothing worked. One fine day, the enterprising woman, accompanied by her chambermaid, knocked on his door. "When Ignatius saw Isabel, he was very astonished, put his head in his hands and said: 'God help me, Roser, you are here? Who brought you here?' She replied 'God and you, my Father.'"[12] Caught in the trap, Ignatius put them up at the House of Saint Martha where they rendered great services. Isabel played at being the Mother Superior, but she wanted more than that. She would not give up until Ignatius integrated her fully into the Society and she could consecrate herself in it by the three vows of religion. Weary of Ignatius beating around the bush, she had recourse to the pope who ordered Ignatius to receive these new recruits. With two other companions, Isabel pronounced her vows on Christmas Day, 1545.

The experiment did not last. Isabel's independent and overwhelming character, her neurotic temperament, the complaints of Jesuits who had never imagined they would work with women, finally wore out Ignatius's patience. He obtained permission from the pope to end this adventure. After a series of stormy meetings where financial questions required the intervention of the tribunal, Isabel finally recognized her mistakes, and renounced her project. Peace and friendship were restored, without rancor, and Isabel would remain faithfully attached to Ignatius until the end of his life.

Notes

1. See Hugo Rahner, S.J. *Saint Ignatius Loyola; Letters to Women* (New York: Herder and Herder, 1960), pp. 114–16. See also Rhodes, "Ignatius, Women, and the *Leyenda de los santos*."

2. Meissner, *Ignatius of Loyola*, pp. 238–47.

3. *Scripta de Sancto Ignatio*, vol. 1, p. 662.

4. *Saint Ignatius's Own Story*, p. 67, num. 97.

5. Instructions to Those Sent on Missions, Rome, 8 October 1552, *Letters and Instructions*, pp. 293–94.

6. Hugo Rahner has counted 139 letters: 89 from Ignatius to various women, and 50 to him (*Letters to Women*, p. 13).

7. See Lisa Fullam, "Juana, S.J.: Status of Women in the Society," *Studies in the Spirituality of Jesuits*, 31/5 (November 1999). See also Gemma Simmonds, C.J., "Women Jesuits?," in *The Cambridge Companion to the Jesuits*, ed. Thomas Worcester, S.J. (Cambridge: Cambridge University Press, 2008), pp. 120–35.

8. Ignatius to Teresa Rejadell, Rome, 18 June 1536, *Saint Ignatius of Loyola Personal Writings*, pp. 129–35.

9. Ignatius to Ponce Cogordan, Rome, 12 February 1555, *Lettrers and Instructions*, pp. 357–41.

10. Ignatius to Jerónima Oluja and Teresa Rejadelel, Rome, 5 April 1549, in Rahner, *Letters to Women*, p. 355,

11. Ignatius to Isabel Roser, Paris, 10 November 1532, in Rahner, *Letters to Women*, p. 267.

12. *Scripta de Sancto Ignatio*, vol. 2, p. 696.

XVIII

THE REFORMER

Because the French cannonball shattered Ignatius's knee in 1521, the same year that Luther was excommunicated, some have seen a sign from heaven in this historical coincidence. This resulted in an excessively narrow interpretation of the work of Ignatius, his teaching, the *Exercises,* and the foundation of the Society as the providential instrument sent by heaven to counter the Reformation, a step many authors were happy to take. Nadal was the first: "The same year that Luther was summoned by the demon, Father Ignatius was summoned by God."[1] For Ribadeneira, there was no doubt that if Luther had been the gravedigger of the faith, Ignatius was its defender. In order to portray an Ignatius called by heaven to oppose Luther and defend the Church, he devoted several chapters of his *Life of Ignatius of Loyola* to describing in extreme and polemical terms the horrors of the Reformation.[2] In a letter written in 1583 to the Father General Claudio Acquaviva (1543–1615), Peter Canisius thanked Divine Providence for inspiring the foundation of the Society of Jesus by Ignatius as troops to combat heresy, as erroneous doctrines were beginning to catch fire throughout Europe.[3] This cliché became so solidly entrenched that the bull of canonization of March 12, 1622, incorporated it.

But Ignatius was not the counterreformer legend such interpreters would have us believe. It was clear that he never read a single line of Luther. In his writings, neither the name of Luther nor Lutheranism ever appears. Ignatius never decided to counter the Protestant Reformation. He was himself a reformer rather than a counterreformer, and he kept his distance from Pope Paul IV, from the party of the *zelanti*, from the Inquisition, from the politics of the Spanish Crown, and from the University of Paris. His project was wider in scope and more fundamental. He wanted to "help souls" without shutting himself into a single task imposed by historical circumstances. His vision swept across a larger horizon in its search for God, in the realization of man's being as a creature. To be sure, he was aware that the Church was in need of reformation, but this task was not incumbent on Jesuits, who were not part of the hierarchy. This reform was the concern of the pope and others responsible for the Church. On the occasion of a conclave to elect a successor to Julius III, Ignatius mentioned this task to the 220 Jesuits in Rome, and asked them to pray that "a good pope who is zealous for the honor of God and the reform of the Church" be chosen. He rejoiced at the election of Marcellus II because he was a pope "concerned with the reform of the Church."[4] This hope was quickly extinguished when the new pope died after a pontificate of twenty-three days. If he trembled upon hearing of the election of his successor, the redoubtable Paul IV, Ignatius could at least hope that the reform would go ahead. How was this reform to be imagined? Gonçalves da Câmara related his opinion: "The Father said that if the Pope were to reform himself, and his household, and the cardinals of Rome, he would have nothing else to do, and everything else would take place subsequently."[5] Even then, reform of the Church passed through the curia.

Ignatius was rightly aware that this Church was not an ideal society, that it needed reform, and that the conduct of some ecclesiastical leaders gave scandal. In spite of that, the Church was guided from on High: "For it is by the same Spirit and Lord who gave the Ten Commandments that our holy Mother Church is ruled and directed."[6] This is why he recommended seeking reasons to defend it rather than attacking it. And the difficulties and harassments that he endured at the hands of ecclesiastical authorities would not make him change his mind.

If he was a reformer, it was along the lines laid down in the *Devotio moderna* movement. Unlike Luther, Ignatius did not attack the hierarchy directly. Instead of denouncing practices and structures, he dedicated himself to helping persons reform their own lives through the *Exercises*. All the same, he did not ignore the debates among those eager for church reform. Sometime before 1535, while he was still in Paris, and, again, at Rome, between 1535 and 1541, Ignatius wrote down some rules "to foster the true attitude of mind we ought to have in the church militant,"[7] rules intended to aid persons doing the *Exercises* who wanted advice as to how they should comport themselves pastorally when in religiously conflicted situations.

Because he was suspected of being a disciple of Erasmus while a student in Paris, Ignatius was careful to keep his distance from the great humanist. In his *Enchiridion*, Erasmus criticized a whole series of pious practices and privileged a purely interior spiritual life. Ignatius, more sensitive to the incarnated dimension of the faith, was wary of this intellectual religion, and of its rejection of any exterior expression of piety. He took up a list of the errors of Erasmus which had been condemned by the Council of Sens, which was held in Paris in 1528, and proposed having a more positive view by praising the practices which the humanist questioned. A rule he formulated—and one often lampooned— posed a question: "If we wish to proceed securely in all things, we must hold fast to the following principle: What seems to me white, I will believe black if the hierarchical Church so defines. For I must be convinced that in Christ our Lord, the bridegroom, and in His spouse the Church, only one Spirit holds sway, which governs and rules for the salvation of souls."[8] Here Ignatius used the very words employed by Erasmus in a quarrel with the theologians of the faculty of Paris. In 1527, Dean Noël Beda (1470–1537) had established a list of errors attributed to Erasmus. The humanist defended himself by accusing Beda of lies, calumnies and defamation. Beda had poured out so many errors, Erasmus wrote, that even if the pope accepted them, it would be necessary to appeal from a pope asleep to a pope awake, because black cannot be made white even if the pope said otherwise. By using Erasmus's expression, Ignatius was not positioning himself on the philosophical level; he did not pretend that black could in fact be white, but was advancing a practical judgment: I should be disposed to accept the authority of the Church.

At Rome, ecclesiastics flirted with the Reformation. Without getting into the theological controversies, Ignatius completed his rules by providing wise advice on ways of dealing with certain questions raised by the reformers. Responsible discourse respected ordinary people with less knowledge and instruction. So he preferred to avoid certain subjects which could do harm by disturbing peace and unity within the Church, and leading astray some of the faithful, e.g., questions concerning predestination, servile fear, the relationship between faith and works, or between free will and grace.[9] When it was a question of justified criticisms, it was better to speak with someone who could remedy the situation rather than troubling people by debating them in the public square.

STRONG-ARM TACTICS

In 1550, ten years after the first confirmation of the Society by Paul III, Pope Julius II confirmed the institute with *Exposcit debitum*. A modification of *Regimini militantis Ecclesiae* reoriented the Society: henceforth Jesuits would not only dedicate themselves to the propagation of the faith, but also to its defense. Thus enemies of the faith were envisaged, which was not the case ten years earlier. Emperor Charles V's victory over the Protestant Schmalkaldic League at Mühlberg in 1547 paved the way for re-Catholization of Protestant regions. The struggle continued until a weary empire granted Protestants some concessions in the 1552 Peace of Passau, concessions formulated into the more famous Peace of Augsburg in 1555. In this much altered religious landscape, emperors, princes, cardinals, and bishops invited Jesuits to found colleges, to lecture at universities, to preach missions, to give retreats, to do all they could to strengthen the faith of Catholics and to prevent further defections to Protestantism.

In a letter to Peter Canisius dated August 13, 1554, Ignatius recommended strongarm tactics against heretics: their exclusion from any public function, confiscation of their property, exile, execution as an example; destruction of their publications, etc. Such unusually extreme proposals demand an explanation. This letter, in fact, reported the conclusions of a debate among Jesuit theologians consulted by Ignatius. Did Ignatius himself endorse these measures? There is room for doubt. A second letter to the same person on the same date tempered this apparent declaration of war. He insisted on a different strategy in the struggle against heresy. Rather than relying on oppression and coercion, he believed it more judicious to strengthen the faith of the people by founding colleges, publishing catechisms and other books which presented the Catholic faith clearly, without forgetting the examples of love, of modesty and of wisdom towards all, even those who are excommunicated.[10]

Contrary to a widely held opinion, Ignatius never relied on the Inquisition to assure the effectiveness of the ministries of the Society, even if he never condemned the tribunal of which he himself had often been the victim. He welcomed the institution of the Inquisition in Rome. But, in general, he preferred to explore other paths of reconciliation, ways more harmonious with "our way of proceeding."[11] The pope had granted to Jesuits faculties to absolve those who recognized their errors; in so doing the pope authorized less intransigent procedures. Nadal summed up these procedures, which the Jesuits should use but which he himself did not always put into practice: dialogue amiably with the interested party and invite mediators who love him; if that did not work, the Jesuit should not run to the bishop to denounce the suspected heretic, but instead speak with the superior and leave the decision in his hands.[12] This is how Ignatius tried to save the Vicar-General of the Capuchins, Bernardino Ochino (1487–1564), who embraced the heresy of Juan de Valdés (c. 1500–1541) in Geneva. In a very emotional letter, full of charity and honesty, he asked Claude Jay, then in Germany, to contact Ochino and encourage him to return to the bosom of the Catholic Church, and to inform him if fear for his person or his interests prevented him from doing so, the Society was ready to help him.[13]

The case of Portugal is enlightening. In 1555, King John III had asked the Jesuits to assume responsibility for the Inquisition within the kingdom.

They had accepted without consulting Ignatius who, when informed, immediately demanded that the promise be suspended until he had made a decision about it. Initially he refused the offer because the vocation of the Society was to help souls through the way of humility. With opposition to the Society in Castile, he was more favorably inclined without, however, making a decision. Perplexed and uncertain, he left the decision to six Jesuits who advised him to accept the king's offer. In a muddled letter, Ignatius sent a confirmation to the Portuguese provincial, Diego Mirón, while simultaneously creating a diversion: on the one hand, he did not want to vex the king, but, since responsibility for the Inquisition did not seem to him to be a task integral to the Society's "way of proceeding," he would prefer that the order come from the pope.[14] In fact, for political reasons, the king's project did not succeed.

NOTES

1. *Nadal*, vol. 5, p. 780. On the Ignatian-Lutheran comparison, see William David Myers, "Ignatius Loyola and Martin Luther: The History and Basis of a Comparison," in Maryks, *Companion*, pp. 141–58.

2. *Life of Ignatius of Loyola*, pp. 118–25, 133–36, 143–44, 178–79, 329–30, nums. 170-78, 190–92, 203, 255, 482.

3. Canisius to Acquaviva, Fribourg, 22 October 1583, in *Beati Petri Canisii, Societatis Iesu, Epistulae et acta*, ed. Otto Braunsberger, S.J. (8 vols., Friburg: Herder, 1896–1923), vol. 8, 176–77. On Canisius and German Protestants, see Hilmar M. Pabel, "Peter Canisius and the Protestants: A Model for Ecumenical Dialogue?,"

Journal of Jesuit Studies 1 (2014), pp. 373–99.

4. Ignatius to Jerómino Doménech, Rome, 24 March 1555, *Letters and Instructions*, pp. 558–59; Ignatius to the Whole Society, Rome, 16 April 1555, *Epistolae et instructiones*, vol. 9, pp. 13–17.

5. *Remembering Íñigo*, p. 196, num. 343.

6. *Spiritual Exercises*, p. 160, num. 365.

7. *Spiritual Exercises*, pp. 157–61, num. 352–70.

8. *Spiritual Exercises*, p. 160, num. 365.

9. *Spiritual Exercises*, pp. 160–61, nums. 366–70.

10. Ignatius to Canisius, Rome, 13 August 1554, *Epistolae et instructions*, vol. 7, pp. 398–404; Loyola to Canisius, Rome,

13 August 1554, *Epistolae et instructiones,* vol. 12, pp. 259–63. The second is translated in *Letters and Instructions,* pp. 504–507.

11. On this distinctive "way of proceeding," see John W. O'Malley, S.J., "Ignatius's Special 'Way of Proceeding,'" in *Saints or Devils Incarnate?,* pp. 117–20.

12. Nadal, *Orationis observationes,* ed. Michael Nicolau, S.J. (Rome: Institutum Historicum Societatis Iesu, 1964), p. 216, num. 726.

13. Ignatius to Jay, Rome, 12 December 1545, *Epistolae et instructiones,* vol. 1, pp. 343–44.

14. *Remembering Íñigo,* pp. 201–202, 206, 210–11, nums. 354, 368, 380–82; Ignatius to Diego Mirón, Rome, 20 June 1555, *Epistolae et instructiones,* vol. 9, pp. 226–27.

XIX

A Very Ordinary Death

Ignatius died from a biliary lithiasis (gallstones) on July 31, 1556. Unlike other founders, he did not publish his last wishes; he did not call his companions to his bedside for a farewell discourse, to confide the future of his work to them, and to bless them one last time; he did not designate a successor; he did not want to finish the *Constitutions* because he did not want the Society to put its confidence in anyone or anything but God. This man who had consecrated his life to serving the Church under the Roman Pontiff did not even receive a papal blessing from Paul IV as he so earnestly desired. Sensing that death was near, Ignatius asked Polanco to go and ask for one. The faithful secretary, occupied with an urgent matter, thought that Ignatius was dramatizing things. He promised to go the following day: "I would prefer today rather than tomorrow; yes, as soon as possible, but do as you see fit, I freely hand myself over to you."[1]

Once again, Ignatius abandoned himself and trusted. Until his last breath, the only thing for him was to have God alone as his refuge. He left Loyola "alone on his mule"; "alone," he set out for Barcelona, to embark "alone" for the Holy Land; "alone and on foot," he had left Spain for Paris in order to salvage his project to study and help souls. At Rome, in his little room, he finished the course of his life "alone." He left this world as does everybody, but with an uncommon abandon and confidence.

At the news of his death, many venerated the body of a man widely admired and already considered a saint. Cardinals, prelates, ecclesiastics of every color, the noble and the poor, all crowded around his coffin to the point where force had to be used to protect his remains from overly zealous devotion.

Ignatius was first buried in the little church of Santa Maria della Strada, which bordered on the house where he lived and worked. In 1587, Father General Claudio Acquaviva had his casket moved to the transept of the new Church of the Gesù where it remains. His tomb was first the object of a furtive cult, then a more public one discreetly advanced by the Society of Jesus eager for the canonization of its founder. Discretion was essential because of new regulations regarding the fostering of cults and the path to canonization. The Society appealed to cardinals, bishops, king, and princes for affidavits and support in its campaign. Three popes, Clement VIII (1536–1605, r. 1592–1605). Paul V (1552–1621, r. 1605–1621), and Gregory XV (1554–1623, r. 1621–1623), received petitions for an official recognition of Ignatius's holiness. The administrative processes dragged on. Finally, on July 17, 1609, the Cardinal Prefect of the Congregation of Rites signed a decree of beatification. After the examination and approbation of ten miracles attributed to his intercession, Ignatius of Loyola was canonized on March 12, 1622, by Pope Gregory XV, the same day as three other Spanish saints, Isidore the Farmer (c. 1070–1130), Teresa of Ávila and Francis Xavier, and one Italian Philip Neri (1515–1595).[2]

Ignatius's cult, unlike that of the apostle of the Indies and Japan or of other saints, is marked by a certain discretion, very much like his life. Because he only desired God's glory, Ignatius liked to hide God's gifts except those that should be manifested for the edification of others. Even if numerous churches bear his name, especially in mission lands where the Jesuits have been active, Ignatius remained an "ordinary" saint. Beyond his death, he still seems to hide himself behind his mission: to bring help to souls. The *Spiritual Exercises* are better known and more frequented than the sanctuaries dedicated to him, and, down through the ages, the Society of Jesus has aroused more interest and curiosity than the person of its founder.

NOTES

1. Juan de Polanco to Pedro de Ribadeneira, Rome, 6 August 1556, *Fontes narrativi*, vol. 1, pp. 764–72.

2. On Ignatius's cause, see A.D. Wright, "'A Race to the Altar': Philip Neri and Ignatius Loyola," in *Leeds Papers on Symbol and Image in Iberian Arts*, ed. Margaret A. Rees (Leeds: Trinity & All Saints' College, 1994), pp. 151–60; A.D. Wright, "'*La sua santità non inclina niente*': the Papacy and the Canonisation of Ignatius Loyola," in McCoog, *Ite inflammate omnia*, pp. 441–55; Simon Ditchfield, "'Coping with the *Beati Moderni*': Canonization Procedure in the Aftermath of the Council of Trent," in McCoog, *Ite inflammate omnia*, pp. 413–39.

Conclusion

We have thus arrived at the end of an adventurous journey in which we have tried to discover the real Ignatius of Loyola behind the ambiguous personage that haunts the popular imagination. We have scrutinized his autobiographical account, heard the immediate witnesses of his life, listened to the reminiscences of his closest companions, read attentively the first official biography, and consulted several specialists.

By rereading his own story in order to ascertain how God had led him, Íñigo set us on an untiring quest for a more effective service of Christ. His first companions have shared with us the enthusiasm and fervor of a group of European students involved in the adventure of founding a new and innovative order. The Roman chronicles of Luis Gonçalves da Câmara, very meticulously updated, introduced us into the daily life of the Superior General of the Society. Conquered by a personality who incarnated the ideals they had in their hearts, along with an unshakeable filial piety, most of these witnesses have painted the portrait of a man who was sovereign and master of himself, the portrait of an ideal superior whose very fits of anger became acts of virtue. Their unrestricted admiration found its expression in the first official biography of Ribadeneira, who had no qualms about fostering hagiographical designs and overlooking whatever could tarnish the halo of the saint to hasten the process of Ignatius's cause. At the risk of endorsing a portrait of an overly gilded legend, it was necessary to confront these testimonies with other points of view—those of his cofounder companions who were just as close to him—who nuance these exaggerated eulogies by evoking traits of an authoritarian, excessive and ambitious character. Their criticisms provided fodder for another legend, a black one. The result is less a photograph of the founder of the

Society of Jesus, and more an impressionistic portrait made up of a multitude of brush strokes, often contradictory, which, as a whole, reveal a personality which is complex, imposing, and very attractive.

Ignatius appears as an ordinary man with the qualities and defects of his people and his times. His deep enthusiasm to follow Christ and his great lucidity regarding himself permitted him to redirect his strong passions to the service of the Church: his ambition, his pride, his need to be admired, his libido, his determination to succeed. In spite of these weaknesses which would persistently resurface in his relations with women and social elites, in the way he exercised authority and demanded obedience or in the manner in which he regulated certain grave internal conflicts, Ignatius was a level-headed leader, full of wisdom, a very reliable discerner, an efficient organizer, and a realistic spiritual guide. An ordinary man, to be sure, but of a holiness which was not very ordinary, who impressed by his balance and by the strength that his personality radiated. His desire to be efficient in Christ's service and to seek the largest benefit, possibly led him to cultivate relations with kings, princes, popes, and other decision-makers, be they politicians or ecclesiastics, without always succeeding in avoiding compromises. Some individuals mistakenly saw ambition and a type of Machiavellianism in all that.

If we look for a defining characteristic which would permit us to come to an overall understanding of the complexity of his person and his work, the concept of "service" immediately comes to mind, with all that this word can evoke of fidelity, courage, self-sacrificing availability and humility. Ignatius of Loyola was essentially a servant, first of the king of Castile, then of Christ and the Church, always wanting to do more to "help souls" everywhere in the world, wherever he would be useful. The mystical grace received on the banks of the Cardoner River had opened his eyes. The world of his time, which had become much larger by the discoveries of new lands and new cultures, is the place where he will serve. He saw the world as a whole, where God is present, active and offered. Without leaving his little room in Rome, Ignatius made his presence felt everywhere that something new was bubbling up in the world, in order to teach people to think for themselves and to take their destiny in hand. By imparting to them his own experience and inviting them to pay more attention to the sensitive and psychological dimension of the person, he opened to them the path of liberty, freedom and personal responsibility. With his *Exercises*, he presented them with an efficient method for discovering the will of God written in their particular circumstances. If his teaching on meeting God beyond all mediation seriously troubled the Inquisition and overly traditional theologians, his insistence on verifying the authenticity of every spirit by its incarnation in a community guaranteed the orthodoxy of his intuitions.

Ignatius of Loyola did not bequeath a theological tradition or a specific philosophy to the Society; rather, he left them a "way of proceeding," an art of approaching people and of resolving issues in four steps: attention to historical circumstances; use of interior experience through discernment; confrontation with reality; and evaluation of decisions taken and questioned. At a time when society was freeing itself from feudalism and organizing itself according to new paradigms, this was a burning issue.

Better than the 1,000 Jesuits divided among thirteen provinces at the time of his death, better than the more than one hundred colleges and houses founded during his lifetime, better than the 7,000 letters addressed to various persons throughout the world, it is evangelical audacity that constitutes the essential of Ignatius's legacy. An audacity which led him to break away from the spirit of his times to bring a more efficient assistance to people who wanted to commit themselves to the service of the Creator without having to leave the world in which they lived and which they loved. By teaching people to make decisions in an autonomous manner, by founding an original order, by insisting on intellectual formation, by promoting the inculturation of the Christian message in the recently discovered lands, Ignatius of Loyola stands out as the great innovator who introduced the Church to modernity.[1]

Ignatius suffered the lot of the pioneers who escape the usual schemas and cannot be conveniently classified according to familiar categories. Because he inaugurated untested ways of evangelizing and had the boldness to violate boundaries forbidden until then, he aroused as much distrust as admiration. He incarnated the most contrary virtues, he has become almost enigmatic and, consequently, troubling. The gilded legend and the black legend have tried to resolve the dialectical tension inherent in his life and his acts, either celebrating a saint too close to heaven or condemning a dangerous Machiavellian strategist. Neither legend allows us to take the measure of the Basque ex-gentleman who became passionate for Christ. In 1640, to commemorate the centennial of the foundation of the Society, the Flemish Jesuits put together a literary cenotaph dedicated to the glory of their founder. A long funeral eulogy, written in an adapted Baroque style, celebrated the virtues of Ignatius. At the center, one sentence, compact to the limit, tries to convey the complexity of the personality of Ignatius. Like a military boundary, it marks the furthest limit where our investigation stops:

Non coerceri maximo,	*Not to be daunted by the most arduous undertaking,*
Contineri a minimo	*Yet also to invest oneself in the smallest*
Divinum est²	*This is divine*

NOTES

1. Maron, *Ignatius von Loyola*, pp. 260–68. See also Moshe Sluhovsky, "Loyola's *Spiritual Exercises* and the Modern Self," in Maryks, *Companion*, pp. 216–31.

2. *Imago primi saeculi Societatis Iesu* (Antwerp: Plantin, 1640), p. 280.

The Life of
Ignatius of Loyola
in Images

The fifteen images that follow are selected from among eighty-one copper engravings executed by Jean-Baptiste Barbé (1578-1649)—who enlisted the young Peter Paul Rubens (1577-1640) to contribute drawings for the project—for the 1609 illustrated biography of St. Ignatius of Loyola (*Vita beati patris Ignatii Loiolae*), published to celebrate his beatification that year by Pope Paul V. The engravings reproduced here are from the copy of this work in the Jesuitica Collection at Saint Joseph's University, Philadelphia. Saint Joseph's University Press commissioned Ursula Hobson to hand-color these engravings to illustrate Father Emonet's biography. Each engraving is accompanied by an English translation, rendered by the late James P.M. Walsh, S.J., of the Latin caption explaining the episode from Ignatius's life that is illustrated. Father Walsh's translations were originally published in the facsimile of the 1609 illustrated Ignatian biography published in 2008 by Saint Joseph's University Press: *Constructing a Saint Through Images: The 1609 Illustrated Biography of Ignatius of Loyola*, with an introductory essay by John W. O'Malley, S.J. As will be obvious to the reader, these engravings and captions represent idealized readings of events in Ignatius' life, which means they do not always represent them accurately.

Militiam sequutus Ignatius, ictu muralis globi crure perfracto à defensione arcis Pampelonæ semianimis excutitur vt seculari militia relicta, ad diuinam se transferat.

2

1. Pursuing a military career, Ignatius is driven from the defense of the fort at Pamplona, half-dead, when a cannon ball strikes the wall and his leg is broken, so that, the worldly army left behind, he might betake himself to God's.

Dum se inuocata diuinæ Matris ope Deo
dicat noctu vigilantem Beatiß.Virgo eiusq;
in gremio puer Iesus illus tri in specie
aliquandiu visi suauissime recreant.

5

2. As he dedicates himself to God, invoking the help of the Mother of
God, and keeps night vigil, the Most Blessed Virgin and the Child Jesus
in her lap, seen for some time in bright appearance, provide sweetest
comfort.

Libellum exercitiorum spiritualium sin-
gulari afflatu Dei, haustaque e
cælo luce conscribit.

21

3. He writes the book of Spiritual Exercises, by a special inspiration of
God and by light drawn from heaven.

Ex Oliueto reuertens ab Armenio custode voce
ac fuste terretur; dumq̃ ne solitarius ea loca pera:
graret, ferociter in hospitium trahitur, inter ea con:
uicia, et contumelias Christum aspicit præeuntem.
28

4. Coming back from Olivet, he is frightened by the Armenian guardian, by his voice and staff, and while, lest he wander through those places all by himself, he is dragged roughly to a hospice amid reproaches and contumely, he sees Christ going before him.

Noctu fusus in preces, quatuor ferme cubitis
elatus a terra, collucente mirum in modum
facie, identidem, crebra inter suspiria inclamat.
O DOMINE SI TE HOMINES NOSSENT!

35

5. At night pouring himself out in prayer, lifted up from the earth almost four cubits, his face lit up in marvelous wise, again and again with many sighs he cries, "O Lord, if only men knew You!"

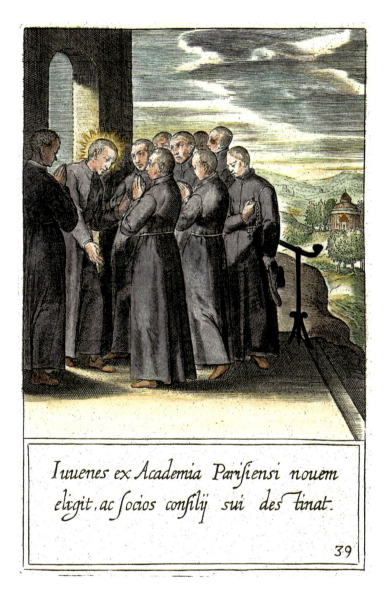

6. He chooses nine young men from the University of Paris and makes
them companions in his plans.

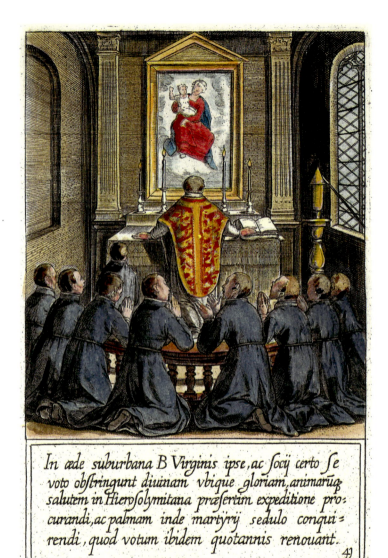

In æde suburbana B Virginis ipse, ac socij certo se
voto obstringunt diuinam vbique gloriam, animarúq;
salutem in Hierosolymitana præsertim expeditione pro-
curandi, ac palmam inde martyrij sedulo conqui=
rendi, quod votum ibidem quotannis renouant.

49

7. In a shrine of the Blessed Virgin on the outskirts of the city [Paris], he
and his companions bind themselves by a firm vow to further the glory
of God and the salvation of souls everywhere, especially by a journey to
Jerusalem, and thus zealously to attain the martyr's palm—a vow they
renew on the same date every year.

8. Returning to Italy, at Venice he welcomes the companions from France, and together with them is inducted into the priesthood; the [ordaining] bishop was so filled with heavenly delight that he foresaw in these new priests naught but something divine.

9. Not far from Rome he entered a deserted church and while he was praying God the Father shows Himself and gives him as companion to His Son as He carries the cross. Likewise, the Son, pronouncing those gentle words, "I will be propitious to you in Rome," welcomes him as companion. Thus the light dawned on Ignatius to call the Society by the name of Jesus.

Paulus III Pont. Max. Societatis Iesu insti= tutum ab Ignatio oblatum postquam legisset, DIGITVS, inquit, DEI EST HIC. socie= tatemque confirmat anno salutis 1540.

56

10. Paul III, Supreme Pontiff, having read the [Formula of the] Institute of the Society of Jesus proposed by Ignatius, says, 'The finger of God is here,' and confirms the Society in the year of salvation, 1540.

Sacramentorum, piarumq̃ concionum vsũ Romæ renouat, ac rationem pueris tradendi doctrinæ christianæ rudimenta Romanis in templis, ac plateis inducit.

60

11. In Rome, he renews the practice of frequenting the sacraments and of giving devout sermons and introduces ways of passing on the rudiments of Christian doctrine to youth in the churches and squares of Rome.

12. Because of Ignatius's special interest in Northern European matters
and his entreaties, Julius III, Supreme Pontiff, founds a college in Rome
for the youth of Germany, no less as an ornament of the Roman Church
than as a bulwark for Germany. (Editor's note: In fact, it was Ignatius
who founded the college. He petitioned Pope Julius to carry the project
forward.)

Societatis Iesu constitutiones frequentibus
Sanctissimæ Trinitatis apparitionibus, atque
illustrationibus. Beatissima item virgine sæpe visa, atq illas approbante conscribit. 65.

13. With frequent manifestations and illuminations of the Most Holy
Trinity and the Blessed Virgin, appearing and bestowing approval on
them, he writes the Constitutions of the Society of Jesus.

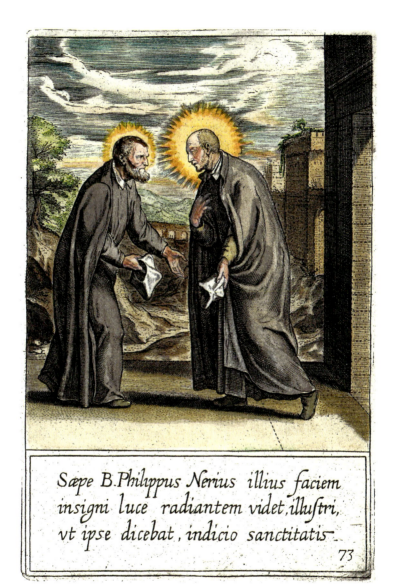

Sæpe B. Philippus Nerius illius faciem
insigni luce radiantem videt, illustri,
vt ipse dicebat, indicio sanctitatis.

73

14. Often Blessed Philip Neri sees his face glowing with a remarkable light—as he would say, a clear indication of sanctity.

*Romæ sanctissime moritur, eodemque
puncto temporis beata eius anima, ingenti
splendore conspicua, Bononiæ a nobili,
sanctaq foemina ferri in coelum aspicitur.*

77

15. At Rome he dies a most holy death, and at that very moment his
blessed soul, outstanding for great splendor, is seen at Bologna by a
noble and holy woman, as if borne to heaven.

Index